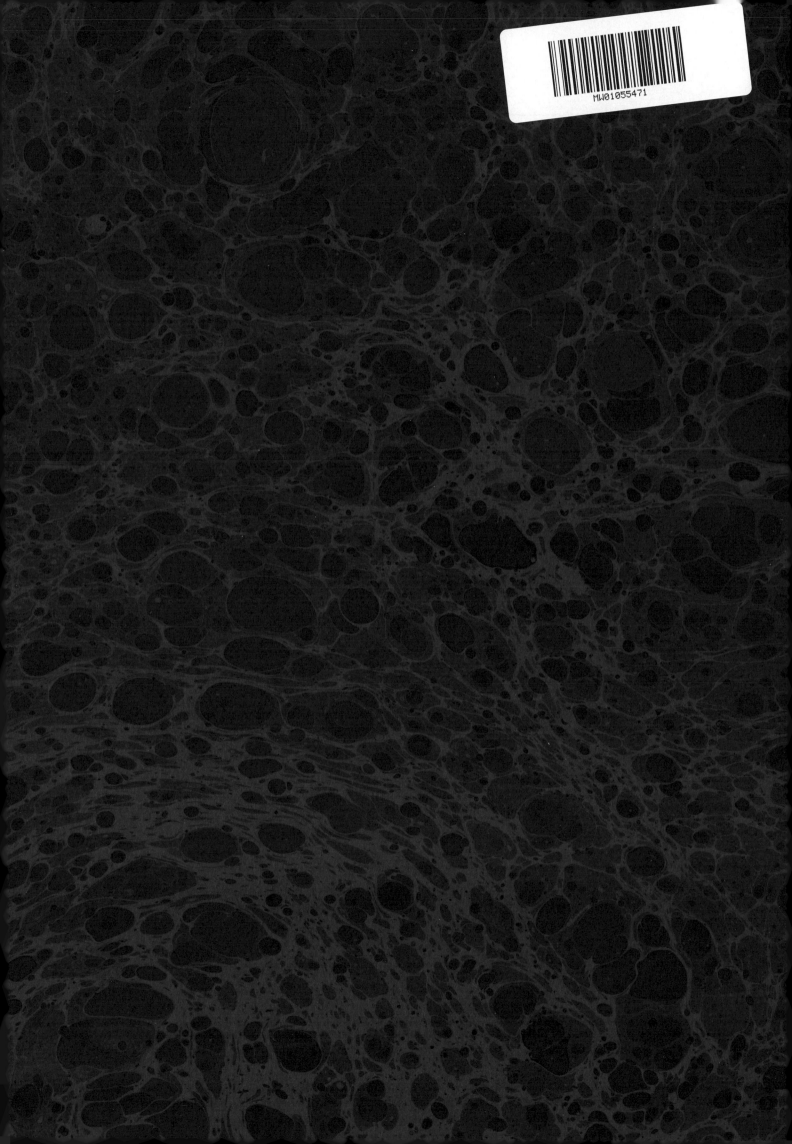

The Enchanted World
# NIGHT CREATURES

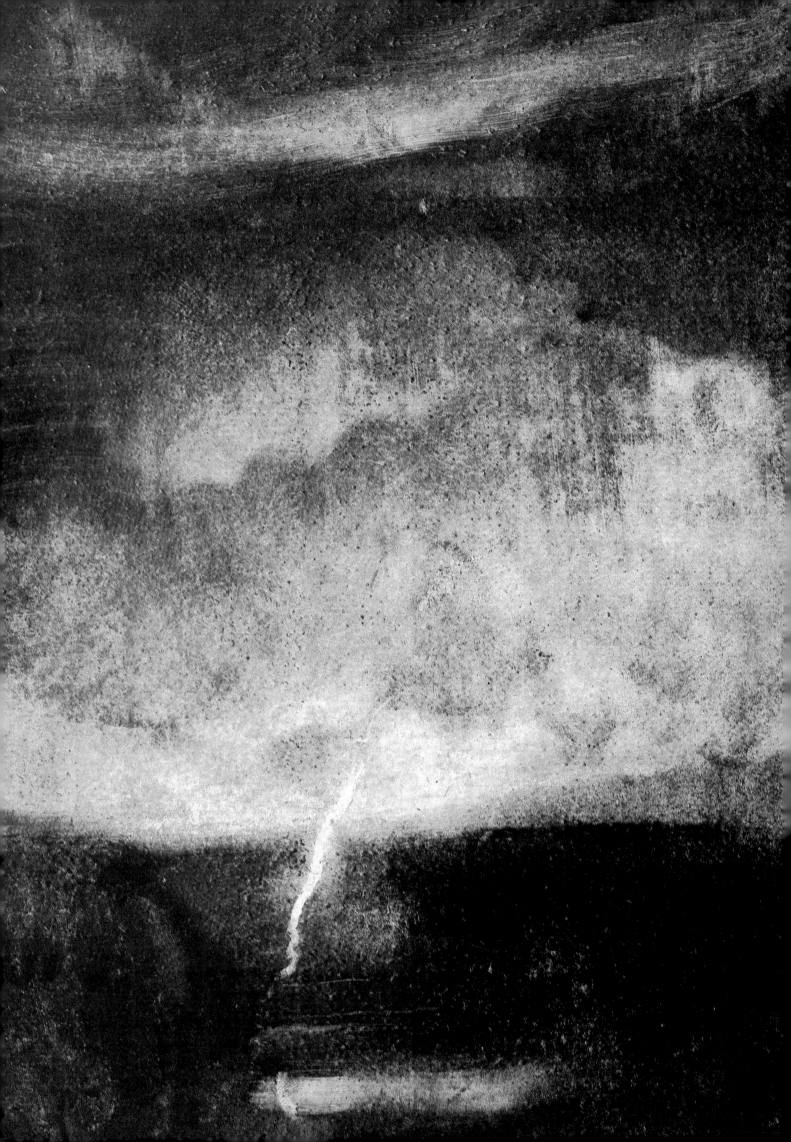

The Enchanted World

# NIGHT CREATURES

by the Editors of Time-Life Books

# The Content

Time-Life Books · Alexandria, Virginia

# Chapter One

# Perilous Paths through the Dark

On its sea-battered Danish island, where moor grasses bowed before the icy blasts of winter winds, the golden-gabled Scylding hall called Heorot was built as a beacon, a lamp to shine through the long northern nights. Within this hall, hearths and torches blazed warm and bright, and drinking horns passed freely among the warriors of the Scylding clan; bards intoned the praises of their chieftain, Hrothgar, the valorous King; harpists sang of warmth and light. Outside the hall, however, solitary in the cold and dark, another kind of being walked.

Although manlike, that being was no man. Huge and hairy, it shambled through the night mists of fell and fen, its claws scrabbling from time to time in the dirt as it tore at its hapless prey—hares, ferrets and other small beasts.

It was old, as old as the making of the world. For unnumbered centuries, it had roamed the land after nightfall, unaware of humankind. Inevitably, however, its attention was attracted to the hall—perhaps by moonlight on the gilded roof, perhaps by the shafts of brightness that shone out across the moor. At length, it made its way across the island and stood outside the towering walls of Heorot, flinching and blinking at the radiance within. Harp music floated in the air. The beast's clawed hands began to curl, and a rumble issued from its throat. A joyless being, it was enraged by the joyful songs of men.

Whether because it feared the light or because some spark of cunning informed its action, the creature waited in the shadow until the singing ceased and the glow from the hearth fires dimmed. When the hall was silent and Hrothgar's warriors lay trapped in dreams on their pallets, it struck, shoving at Heorot's great doors. With a groan, they gave way. Into the dim chamber the huge form lurched, its head swinging from side to side, its nostrils flaring at the human scent.

It feasted then, grasping the warriors in it talons, crushing the bodies, tearing at sinews and cracking bones in its jaws. At last, when the hair at its gaping mouth was matted with blood, it returned to the darkness. For the moment, the beast was sated, but it dragged two victims away to its lair. The rest were left where they lay, gruesomely mangled. A few fortunate men had huddled unnoticed in corners of the hall and survived to tell the tale.

Thus began the siege of Heorot, a horror that endured for twelve long years. On random nights the creature attacked, brutally squeezing the life from warriors within the hall. No man could resist such strength; no weapon could do the beast harm. Its power and cruelty were of a measure beyond human experience.

Soon the island roads were lined with grave mounds. Hrothgar's remaining warriors dared come no more to Heorot. At night they huddled in their own lesser halls, locked in with their sheep and cattle, fearing to venture abroad. Golden Heorot lay dim and cold, abandoned save for the creature that clumsily capered there on moonless nights. The Scyldings called this being Grendel, a name that meant "grinder."

Word of the Scyldings' woe — of the weakening of the warriors and the destruction of the kingdom — spread to distant shores. Most men shunned the island, but one sought it out. He arrived clad in mail and bearing noble arms. Fourteen companions, warriors all, came with him.

The watchman at the shore who challenged the stranger when his longship grated onto the shingle recognized his name. So did Hrothgar when it was given. The newcomer was Beowulf, a young lord of the Geatish kingdom to the east; his name, "bee wolf," for "bear," signified his enormous strength. In him, valor, comeliness and charity were present in a way that set him apart from other men. Beowulf was a hero, a light to the people in a dark age.

He had come to battle Grendel. So he told Hrothgar, and the Scylding King honored him for his courage. Once more,

hearth fires blazed in Heorot and their smoke, rising through holes among the rafters, blew like flags in the evening air. Once more, men feasted on venison and the thick round loaves of bread that people ate then. Once more, as in the old days, Hrothgar's Queen walked among the warriors, offering each the golden drinking horn. Once more, harp song drifted out from the echoing mead hall and across the wind-swept moors.

But when the feasting was done and the harper ceased his singing, the Scyldings withdrew to safer quarters and left the place to Beowulf. He saw that the fires were banked and that his men were disposed around the lofty chamber on pallets to sleep. Then he unlaced his shirt of chain mail and set it aside with his helmet and sword, knowing that the creature could not be harmed by human weapons. It must be fought with sinew and muscle alone.

Beowulf set himself to face the darkness. He wrapped himself in his cloak and lay down near the hearth. The fire glow faded; the rafters disappeared in gloom. He listened intently for any sound that might herald the approach of the beast, but he heard nothing except an occasional rustle among the embers and the slow breathing of his fellows.

The attack came in a blast of wind, with no more warning than a shudder that traveled through the earthen floor of the hall. The doors slammed open like thunder, and a shadow loomed black against the sky outside the hall, blotting out the stars. With a swiftness that amazed Beowulf, the creature seized the man nearest the door. Before the victim could cry out, his throat was torn open and his spine snapped by the great claws. Beowulf, seeing that he could do nothing, remained still, feigning sleep even though the others had leaped up. Perhaps to deal with the easiest foe first, Grendel turned and bent to Beowulf where he lay. Then the Geatish warrior, wound like a spring by the hours of waiting, moved, taking the beast by surprise. Eluding the creature's grasp, he locked one of its hands in his own iron grip, bending the blood-slicked claws back against the wrist. Grendel writhed, howled, and tried to pull away, but Beowulf was too strong.

In the death-battle that followed, benches crashed to the ground and embers scattered, setting tiny fires in the hall. The Geatish warriors circled the straining combatants, seeking an opening for a thrust. But whenever they struck, their blades merely glanced off Grendel's hide. With his bear's strength, Beowulf still held the enemy's hand, twisting as Grendel pulled. Finally the arm crackled and broke, and white bone tore through the flesh of the massive shoulder. And still Grendel lurched and jerked. Suddenly the flesh ripped again, and black blood spouted as the arm tore free. Wailing as its life drained away, the beast stumbled out into the darkness, seeking its lair.

In the mead hall, Beowulf stood sweating and swaying, still holding the clawed arm of Grendel. Then he and his men hung the bloody prize from the highest gable of Heorot, and they summoned the Scyldings to witness the triumph.

The next night, Heorot rang with laughter and singing, and the Scyldings slept once more under the carved rafters. But the rejoicing came too soon. In the morning, one man was gone. A blood-flecked track in the dirt outside showed that he had been dragged away. Some bestial killer still lived.

Old warriors said that it was Grendel's dam, come to take a life for a life. While the she-beast survived, raging for vengeance, there was no safety for mortals in the dark hours. Therefore, with Hrothgar and a troop of warriors, Beowulf set out to find Grendel's parent.

The company rode far from the fields and fortress of the Scylding King. Across the moors they traced the bloody trail, sunlight glinting on the bronze fittings of their wooden shields and on their golden helmets. The track led into rocky highlands, where cold winds carried the moans of wolf song to them. At last they came to a halt beside a lake.

Dimness reigned here. The lake, fed by icy mountain torrents, spread gray under a weeping sky. Black cliffs fringed it, and ancient ash trees, crusted with lichen and stiff with hoarfrost, grew along the shore. On slimy ledges and in the water, serpents flashed and coiled. Bits of flesh bobbed on the surface, and the air was heavy with the odor of decay.

The horses backed and shied; the hounds whined and cringed; and fear stirred in the hearts of the warrior company. A few of the men knew the lake, having come across it in the course of a hunt. They spoke of it with wonder and dread, saying that a stag they had pursued to this spot chose the mercies of the hunt-

*As mindlessly murderous as her offspring, Grendel's dam*
*was slain in her bone-littered cave by the Geatish hero Beowulf.*

ing pack rather than plunge into those evil waters and swim for freedom.

Beowulf did not reply to their tale or even seem to hear. He said to a kinsman: "If I die by this, give my greetings and my gold to my King. And serve as protector for my companions in my place."

He dismounted, stood a moment at the lake edge as if in contemplation, then dived. No man followed. Beowulf later told how he had descended and how, lungs bursting, he had been caught by clawed hands at the mouth of a deep cave and dragged inside. There he had seen the one-armed body of Grendel and the grim harvest of human bones around it. He turned to face that body's guardian. His own sword was useless against her, he knew. But another sword, large and gleaming, hung on the cave's wall – giants' work, he said, and deadlier than any mortal weapon. He seized it and, with a single whistling stroke, killed her.

His companions had presumed him dead, although his past deeds were such that they clung to hope long past the time when any ordinary mortal would have drowned. Then one man gave a shout, and all stared at the waters, now stained with blood. A golden helmet broke the surface, and Beowulf emerged. In his hand he bore a trophy: the severed head of Grendel. The depredations of the night beasts on the Scyldings' island were forever ended.

But Beowulf's fame would outlast many lifetimes. Over and over, chroniclers told how a mighty warrior, alone, defeated the powers of darkness. Because of his courage, his name lived for a thousand years.

His triumph was all the greater because of the rawness of the world he lived in. The earth was closer to its beginnings then, and old powers, many of them malignant, still

*Born of primal Chaos, the Greek goddess Nyx soared across the sky each night,*
*draping the heavens with her black veil and bejeweling her trail with stars.*

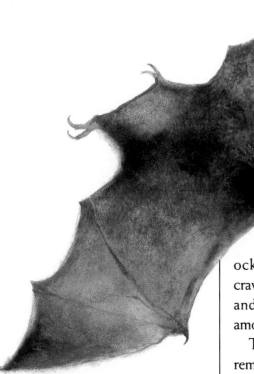

## A winged emblem of evil

Swooping and swerving as they hunted by night, bats struck fear in the hearts of humankind. They were furred like beasts yet winged like birds – an in-between nature believed to link them to old magic. Some folk said that bats were the ghosts of the unburied dead, or of criminals or those who trafficked with devils. Others concluded that they were witches in disguise, or even cloaks for Satan himself when he went traveling.

People who were bold enough (or foolish enough) to deal with the forces of darkness attempted to put bats' bodies to use. Witches reportedly included the blood of bats in the ointments that enabled them to fly. Slavic men wore dead bats suspended from their necks, thinking that emanations from the little corpses would arouse desire in women. And in the Austrian Tyrol, it was said that a person who acquired a bat's left eye could become invisible at will.

throbbed with hidden life. Night, in particular, brought them forth and allowed them to flourish. Out of profound depths, from forest and sea, from hillock and cave, from rock and shadow crawled creatures of the nocturne, a cruel and ghastly host searching for victims among intruding humankind.

These beings were vestiges of chaos, remnants of a formless time older than human reckoning. They survived many centuries into the era of humankind, preying on the latecoming race in a variety of ways. Some, like Grendel, seethed with hatred for the intruders and assaulted them in a frenzy of destructiveness. Some were unable to cross human thresholds and had to wait for unwary victims who ventured abroad at night. Some invaded human bodies and turned their hosts into nightstalking animals; these were called werebeasts. Some invaded the bodies of the dead and transformed the corpses into terrible beings that gnawed human flesh and drank human blood.

All were sons and daughters of darkness, freed only after the sun had set and blackness crept across the land. It was no wonder that mortals held those hours in fearful contemplation. They knew the night for what it was – the living shadow of the dark age before the earth took shape.

Whenever people sang of beginnings, they sang of primal night. Before the creation of life, they said, there was only uncomprehending darkness and the borderless void. In ancient Egypt, wise men wrote that the world emerged from an endless waste of gloom-shrouded seas. Nomadic Hebrews and Phoenician sailors said that, at time's beginning, nothing existed except a black and windy weltering. The first act of creation, all agreed, was the making of light to drive away the dark.

But some of that primal darkness endured. Night was its relic, its memory. People saw divine strife in the alternation of dark and light: In Scandinavia, for instance, night was the goddess Nôtt, riding the skies in a chariot until she disappeared beyond the horizon, forced down by the power of her son, Day. The froth from her horse's mouth fell to the earth as dew.

In Greece, the night goddess – first child of Chaos – was called Nyx. Darkly fecund, she gave birth to a host of terrors. Doom and disease, pain and strife, sorrow and old age were her children, and she was the mother of those same-seeming twins, death and sleep. All this fearful brood she engendered so that they might rule the yet-unborn race of humankind. But ultimate power was retained by Nyx, a winged deity who, as each day approached its close, drew a black veil across the sky and flew free in the heavens, trailed by a retinue of stars.

As centuries passed, of course, people ceased talking in terms of these fancies. Yet even in the age of mighty palaces and soaring cathedrals, of well-tilled fields and thriving villages, the dread of night remained undiminished. By day, the world presented an orderly picture: In the shadow of bristling castle towers, linen-smocked farmers, attended by flocks of greedy crows, plowed and sowed and harvested; white-wimpled goodwives tended their hearth pots; blacksmiths worked their forges; children played in the fields.

But that cheerful order began to dissolve each afternoon when the shadows lengthened. In the twilight, all made for shelter. The crows gave their last, harsh calls and took wing for their woods. Lowing cattle, their bells clanking dully, were driven into their byres. Grandmothers herded flocks of geese to the haven of pens. Then the curfew sounded, tolled by a bell or called by a horn, and lords and ladies retreated to their fortresses and dropped the gates. Farmers, wives and children returned to their cottages, shut the doors, latched them and threw the bolts across for safety.

The darkness that blanketed the turning world in those days is hard to envision now. The night sky then was an ebony canopy crowded with stars and banded by the Milky Way, a pale river of light so familiar and easily seen that the British called it Watling Street, after their own Roman road. Through this sparkling tapestry sailed the radiant moon. When it was at the full, even the smallest blade of grass on earth shone sharp and clear; when it waned or was obscured by clouds, a man could not see his hand in front of his face.

This nighttime realm was almost unbroken by mortal-made light. A bird flying over Europe would see a landscape of almost unrelieved black and gray. A few points of brightness might shine in coastal regions; these were beacons for sailors. In towns might appear moving rows of illumination that signified torchlight processions. There were no street lights, except at crossroads near cities.

And what of the people in their houses? The rich and royal had beeswax candles or, more frequently, candles made of quicker melting tallow – clarified animal fat, usually mutton. Tallow candles had to be snuffed and trimmed every few minutes because the fat melted and ran so rapidly. Lesser folk had smoky little lamps – shallow vessels of earthenware or bronze that held fish or olive oil and floating wicks of twisted fiber for burning. The lamps stank and dripped, and their light diminished quickly as the oil was consumed. People also had rushlights, peeled rushes dipped in fat and held horizontal by pincer devices. These left a greasy line of drippings below them as they burned.

All such devices and makeshifts yielded pitiable illumination in the vast, embracing night. So feeble were they as a counterweight against the dark that most people chose to sleep when daylight failed.

Still, there were people who braved the late hours to travel on the open road. Some were merchants, who followed a circuit of markets and fairs, their pack mules and carts laden with wool and hides. Some were troubadours and jongleurs, minstrels who wandered from court to court. Some were soldiers, returning weary from the innumerable wars of the time. And many were pilgrims whose cloaks were festooned with lead or tin badges and shell brooches – souvenirs of the shrines they visited, such as that of Our Lady of Walsingham in England or the shrine of

Unwise was the wayfarer who continued his journey
by night. In the shadows cast by cold moonlight,
greedy eyes glittered, claws curled, teeth clicked.

St. James of Compostela in faraway Spain. All these travelers passed through hard and lonely country. The few highways, usually remnants of ancient Roman roads, were of uncertain repair. And highways quickly dwindled to commoner track roads, where a man had to stand aside when ox-drawn wagons passed. Connecting these thoroughfares to isolated hamlets and farms was a network of tiny footpaths, each no wider than an armspan. The roadways were difficult at the best of times; they were all but impassable in snow or rain. In good conditions, a traveler would be lucky to walk twenty miles in a day.

The Church had hostels for its itinerant children, but these were widely scattered, and it was inevitable that travelers should sometimes find themselves alone on moor or mountain when the sun dipped in the west and the trees threw long shadows across the ground. The air would grow still and chill as darkness fell; the traveler would pull up his hood and kindle the flame he carried in his cresset – an iron fire basket – or horn lantern, to light his way until the moon rose and shone on his path.

The wayfarer's other defenses against mischance were slight. If he was wise, his walking staff was made of rowan – mountain ash. The rowan was the Northmen's ancient World Tree, the source of life and guardian of humankind. Travelers also clung to certain objects that recalled the light of day, hoping that these might cast day's grace on them and shield them from the dark. Among such charms was the field-grown daisy – the cherished "day's eye" of the British, which opened its petals to the sun each morning and closed them again at nightfall. Another charm was St.-John's-wort, picked on Midsummer Eve, or Saint John's Eve. This herb's flower resembled a miniature sun; hence it was known as *sol terrestris*, or "terrestrial sun." Still another plant was the four-leaf clover, whose green disks echoed the shape of the Christian Cross; to be useful, the clover had to have been found by the person who bore it, picked in secret and sewed into the traveler's cloak hem or tucked inside his shoe. A crust of bread – the staff of life – guarded against peril, too. As the rural saying had it, "That holy piece of bread charms the danger and the dread."

If these talismans were efficacious and the traveler was fortunate, he heard nothing as he walked at night but his own footsteps in the dirt, the crackle of his lantern flame, the occasional hooting of an owl, and the scufflings of badgers and snufflings of hedgehogs – the homely sounds of nocturnal animals going about their business. He would see little besides his lantern's tremulous light on the dark path ahead and, when the moon rose at last, the silvered leaves and branches of the trees. But if his journey took him to a crossroads, he was likely to find reminders of his danger. A crossroads was an in-between place – neither one place nor another – and because of this ambiguousness, a route that alien beings might take into the mortal world. To forfend such an invasion, people often erected a small stone pillar at the spot, a kind of outdoor

*Attended by ghostly throngs, Hecate, ancient Queen of dark and death, left her nether world nightly to terrify travelers. Such was her power that even the earth trembled at her approach.*

altar piled with sacrifices – black puppies and ewes, fish and eggs, milk and honey, garlic cloves. These offerings were known as Hecate's Supper, and they were meant to placate the wrath of the eldest and most vicious of night creatures.

Hecate was a pagan moon-goddess so powerful that fear of her cruel ways extended even into Christian times. Keeper of the keys to hell, she was called the Mother of Witches and the Queen of Ghosts. The Greeks styled her Agriope – or "Savage Face" – and indeed, the sight of her struck terror into the doughtiest heart.

Her approach was heralded by the distant howling of wolf packs and sometimes the screaming of the winds, for Hecate was a storm bringer. Then, as if the veil that covered chaos had been rent, allowing the wayfarer a glimpse into the remote past, she would rise terribly from the crossroads, a monstrous woman with snake-infested hair. Sometimes she was three-headed and bore a sword and torch aloft. Always, she was enveloped by pale, gibbering, writhing spirits of the dead, whom she released each night to haunt the world, and by weasels, owls and a pack of hellhounds. The whole screaming mass would ascend into the sky, a swirling stain upon the heavens. The traveler, rendered lightless when storm-gusts extinguished his lantern, would be driven mad by the sight.

But Hecate was rarely seen as the centuries rolled by: A cosmic being, she withdrew from the petty world of humankind. Far more common were lesser creatures that attached themselves to particular places – lonely roads, hills and woods. Only mortals who trespassed on their territories were likely to encounter them.

Many night creatures of this sort had names derived from the Welsh *bwgwl*, or "object of terror." In northern England and on the Scottish border, such creatures were called bogles, bugaboos, boggarts; in Cornwall, they were bucca-boos. The French spirit was known as the *bugibus*, the German creature as a *Boggelmann*. These beings were usually shadowy and dark. Most could change shape at will – perhaps appearing as a large black dog or a sack of grain – and so were difficult to describe. Generally, they were harmless, although their aimless trickery could be hard on nerves stretched thin by the gloom.

The folk of a farming hamlet near Ebchester in Northumberland told of a prank played on an elderly woman who stayed out late in the twilight, gleaning small sticks for kindling. As she bent to pick up a branch, she spied at the edge of the path a neatly tied sheaf of straw. Being a thrifty woman, she gathered the sheaf into her apron and set off for home.

She walked slowly because of her age, and when the last light failed, she walked more slowly still, for the bundle in her apron grew heavier and heavier until it pulled at the stitching of her sash. At last, she loosened the apron corner to tip the burden out. Out it came, but of its own volition. Seeming to sprout flapping arms and legs, it hopped and shuffled down the path and into the woods, hooting and cackling maniacally all the while. As for the old woman, she simply chuckled when she had caught her breath. She had been a victim of her hamlet's own particular bogle, a shape-shifting trickster called the Hedley kow, after the name of the place.

Bogles remained more of a nuisance than anything else. They even had a certain usefulness: Their names could be used as threats to prevent children from straying. But certain other night creatures, which, like the bogles, attached themselves to lonely places and had the ability to shift in shape, were not at all amusing.

These beings waited for wayfarers and, with a kind of insane malevolence, turned the humans into beasts of burden. A man walking along a road would suddenly stagger as a night spirit mounted his back. Its weight was immense, and there was no hope of shaking the creature off, for it dug long claws into the traveler's shoulders and face to maintain its seat. Breathing miasma, it crooned abuse into the traveler's ear. Sometimes the sound of church bells or the break of day could dislodge it, but before that happened, the victim might die of exhaustion. Such a spirit was named Kludde in Belgium, Oschaert in Scotland, and called *Aufhocker* – meaning "leap upon" – in Germany.

*C*reatures worse than these – creatures like Grendel, but not so far-ranging – roamed wild places once, and their names conjured deep dread. On the Scottish coast not far from the Isle of Skye, a being called the Headless Trunk patrolled during the small hours; it never touched wandering children or their mothers, but men who crossed its territory in the dark would be found horribly mutilated the next day. And to the south, in Leicester, Black Annis walked.

Said to be a descendant of an ancient, bloodthirsty goddess, Black Annis was one-eyed, livid-faced and long-clawed. She haunted the Dane Hills and, at twilight, crouched in an oak tree. This tree, the last vestige of a forest that had covered the land before history began, evidently gave her special shelter. She waited patiently for passersby, but her special victims were children. These she flayed alive with her curving claws. The tender flesh she ate, but the pathetic little skins she took to a cave in the hills – known, with mordant humor, as Black Annis' Bower – to hang on cold stone walls as trophies of a triumph of the old world over the new.

Yet the ordered realm of creation had one power that Black Annis and her fellows could not withstand: light. At cock's crow, when the east began to glow and birds resumed their chatter, the army of the night was forced to retreat. Loping and shuffling, crawling and scuttling, its grim soldiery sought safety beneath the earth. Those caught by daylight suffered for it.

For minor bogles, the sufferings seem to have been distressing, but not particularly severe. These creatures simply lost their powers. The Shetland Islands off Scotland, for instance, once were haunted by trows, gnarled little night beings known to inflict disease on mortals and to kidnap their infants. Trows moved so lightly and swiftly in the darkness that mortals rarely saw more of them than fleeting shadows. If the trows failed to reach their own shelters by dawn, however, they became prisoners of the light, for their gateways closed at daybreak. This was once witnessed by three young Shetland peat cutters working late in the day in an island bog.

It was a fluttering movement that first attracted their attention: A tiny, wizened woman, gray of skin and clothed in gray rags, wandered distractedly at the edge of the turf. She appeared to be searching for something: She bent, she stooped, she knelt from time to time and put her ear to the ground. Always, she chittered to herself in unintelligible, birdlike chirps.

The youths recognized her for what she was—a day-bound trow. The entrance to her shelter had disappeared at dawn, and she was trapped on earth in full human view. The peat cutters gave her a wide berth at first, but one of them, overcome with curiosity, finally tried for a closer examination. Setting down his knife and spade, he walked gingerly toward the trow, keeping her always in sight, which was difficult, because she continued to scamper and duck and whimper.

He moved too slowly. As he neared the little creature, the sun dropped behind the horizon. At that instant, the earth seemed to shudder, and the little creature, spying the portal to her subterranean home, vanished.

The Shetland trows were relatively minor bogles; some varieties even served the mortals who shared their islands. Possibly this was why daylight deprived them of their magic but not of their lives. The daylight fate of their Scandinavian cousins—called night trolls or ramblers—was more severe, perhaps because those creatures

were unrelievedly evil. Humans were as toys to them: These haunters did murder and worse than murder, simply for sport.

Night trolls stayed hidden in caves by day, but when all traces of light disappeared, they emerged to scour the dark pine forests and the fjords for human prey. Long-armed and powerful, they were covered with earth and moss. Their eyes bulged, their loose mouths gaped and drooled, and their swollen noses twitched at the scent of human blood, for trolls were creatures wrought of cold, and the heat of humanity warmed their flesh.

Trolls did not always kill and devour their victims: They had other uses for humankind. A woman seized in a troll's claws and dragged to its cave might find herself forced into slavery, trapped forever in the foul-smelling earthen den to cook human bones and gobbets of flesh brought back by the creature from its nightly ramblings. Worse, she might be made to serve as the creature's wife. And after months of abuse, of pinching and tugging by the troll, of merciless beration, or rubbings with strange and stinging ointments, she would begin to lose her human nature. Her face would crease and darken; her nose would grow broad and bulbous and pitted; her once-fair skin would sprout coarse, matted hair; and her voice would deepen to gutteral grunts. Never again would she bask in the pale northern sunlight. Never again would she know a mortal man's love, for troll wives, whether or not they had ever been human, were as greedy and lecherous as their loathsome mates, and as feared.

Trolls possessed strength far exceeding that of most mortals, yet—as in the case of

*Haunter of Scottish byways, a headless human trunk guarded the lands of the McDonalds of Morar. Women and children it ignored, but male wanderers died in its strong hands.*

Grendel—mortals sometimes fought them. Not all their challengers were lordly warriors such as Beowulf. One, who dwelled in Iceland, was an outlaw.

His name was Grettir, Asmund's son, called the Strong, and he was born in Biarg in the western part of the island. As a youth, he was fearless and famed for his fighting prowess. All went well for him until he killed a walker—a murderous ghost that animated the body of a corpse. Dying, the creature cursed the man; the curse bit, and Grettir's luck turned. Not long after, he was falsely accused of murder and sent to wander, an outcast, far from the settlements of his fellows.

For many years, Grettir walked the wilds alone, taking shelter where he could and learning to live off the scant provender of the icy wastes. One year at the winter solstice—the time when nights are longest and days shortest—Grettir found himself beset by a storm. The wind screamed, the snow blew thick and stinging. Ice crusted Grettir's beard and clogged his nostrils. His eyes watered with the cold, and the tears froze on his cheeks. Yet he bent his head and trudged stolidly on. He had no choice.

A black shape loomed suddenly out of the snow. He halted and drew his knife with stiff fingers, for this season of darkness held many dangers. When the shape remained motionless, Grettir advanced cautiously. Then, with rueful amusement, he saw that it was a fence post and had a mate: He was at the gate to a farm. A house lay ahead, barely visible through the blizzard. He gained it and pounded on the door. A woman's voice asked his name.

Because he was an outcast and might be turned away even on this bitter night, he shouted above the howling of the wind: "I am Guest, a wanderer seeking shelter."

At once, the thudding of the bolt sounded and the door swung open. Grettir ducked his head under the low lintel and strode in, blinking a little in the light.

This evidently was a prosperous farm. The woman who had admitted him wore a gown and kirtle of fine, heavy wool, banded with embroidery. The room he stood in had whitewashed walls and a deep hearth where a fire blazed high and a steaming pot hung. The tables and benches were richly carved; a massive loom stood in one corner. Low doors showed rooms beyond, and he could hear the murmuring of servants.

But the woman who greeted him had no welcoming smile, although she gave him words of welcome, such as they were. "The house is yours," she said, "and anything in it you may want. But as for protection, that you must provide yourself."

"What is this?" said Grettir. "Where is the master of the house?" She made no reply until she had him settled by the fire and provided with food and ale. Then she told him her story.

The farm was called Sandhaugar, or "Sandheaps," and once it had been prosperous indeed. Now good folk avoided it, and not even half the fields were tilled. The place was troll-haunted. Two years before, at the time of the winter solstice, the woman's husband had been taken in the night. The next year, again at the sol-

*By many a rural road lurked the night fiends known as dark riders. They sprang upon the backs of travelers, clawing with cruel hands and scorching with fiery breath.*

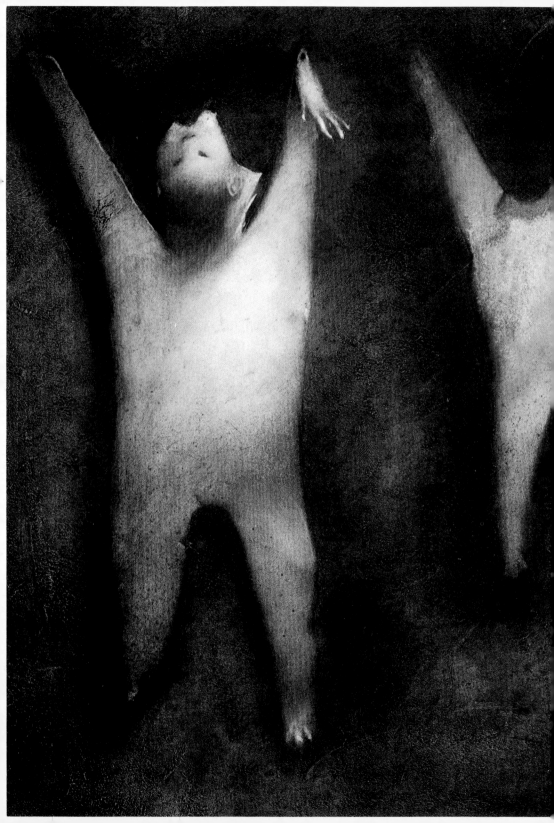

The hills of Leicester were haunted by the hag Black Annis, a remnant of an
old world and enemy of the new. Beneath a gnarled oak tree lay her cave,
walls adorned with the skins of little children who had ventured too near.

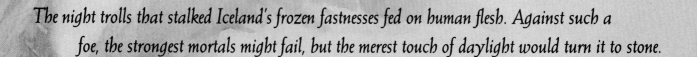

stice, his housecarl, or steward, had gone as well, with nothing but a pool of blood by the door to show that he had lived. Now the woman awaited the troll's return, and she had no one to defend her.

But Grettir, having fought a corpse, had no fear of living trolls, and he was prepared to aid this woman.

The next day was the day of the Yule celebration; the few hours of sunlight shone red and calm. He sent the widow, with two of her servants, to a kinsman at a nearby farm. The other servants were told to stay in back rooms, barricaded from within by boards and logs. When the early twilight fell, he spread a pallet for himself in the front chamber. He banked the fire, set a single rushlight burning by the door, and settled down to wait.

He waited thus for hours, replacing the rush as it burned itself out. Midnight passed, the coals in the fire grew cold, and the dark hours slid toward morning. Finally he heard the shuffling footsteps of the haunter of the farm and the scrabbling of its fingers at the doorframe.

With a splintering crash the door fell open. Grettir's adversary lurched into the room, all but filling it. The intruder was a troll wife. Her enormous head lolled crazily on her humped shoulders. Her blood-veined eyes rolled. Lumpish excrescences, stiff with hair, sprouted from her cheeks and nose. In huge hands she bore a meat cleaver and a chopping trough. She had come prepared for butchery. She dropped them when Grettir rose, his knife in his hand. Then she lunged at him. Such was her strength and quickness that she pinioned him and

forced him out of the warm chamber into her own territory, the out-of-doors, where darkness and cold reigned.

Across the snowy yard they struggled, panting and grunting, across icy fields to the river that watered the farm, and finally to a rocky ledge where a half-frozen fall tumbled to the riverbed below. The troll snarled and jabbered, dragging Grettir onto the slippery rocks. With a mighty effort, he upset her balance, and at that instant, he shoved his knife into her shoulder. The troll wife screamed. Just then, the sun appeared at the rim of an eastern ridge. Grettir felt strength returning to his arms.

But he did not need it. With a hoarse cry, she released him. Her great bulk swelled, until her eyes were black and her skin taut and shiny. Then she burst in a blinding spray of blood. Slowly, the loose skin collapsed and crumpled toward the rock edge, shriveling into a boulder that still bore the troll wife's face, its mouth wide in a silent scream. Trolls could not survive the sun. It turned them to stone.

As for Grettir, always a wanderer, he went on to other adventures, but people told the tale of his bravery again and again. And from settlements up and down the river, people came for centuries to see the stone troll frozen above the falls, sentenced to watch with blind eyes each new day's dawning for as long as there was sun to rise.

# A Reckoning with the Fianna's Ancient Bane

When Cormac Mac Art was High King of Ireland, his seat at Tara was the heart of the country and proof against any human foe, yet it was a frail barrier against the creatures of the dark. Set on a grassy hill, the fortress loomed above a spreading plain. Within its walls stood seven great wooden halls for the household of the High King and for the warriors who defended it — the knights of the Fianna, of all Irishmen the bravest and the best. Quick and strong were these men, well tested and well trained; they kept the King's peace in all the Irish provinces. Yet once a year on a certain night, even the Fianna were made helpless as children and useless as dead men.

The one night was Samain, the flicker of time when autumn had ended and winter not yet begun; on that night, the beings of darkness were free to roam, and the High King's household barred the gates of the fortress against them. The warriors of the Fianna hung their shields in the banqueting hall and feasted together. Their voices were merry, but their eyes were watchful.

Watchfulness did them little good. When the winter moon began its journey across the heavens, a shadow — man-shaped, but no man — appeared on the plain, moving slowly toward Tara. In its arms it bore a harp whose strings gave forth a melody that curled over the walls and into the fortress. And wherever the notes were heard, the mortal listeners slept.

Then the shadow-man struck: Unopposed, it slid over the walls and into the banqueting hall. From its mouth came blasts of flame that ignited the pillars and exploded among the roof beams. Some warriors died in the gusts of fire; some awakened from the spell and escaped, for the creature vanished with its magic harp when the flames rose high.

Those who glimpsed it—a blackness dancing against the scarlet light—knew it from tales they had heard all their lives. The creature was Aillen, a restless remnant of an elder race, long ago forced by mortals into the other world beneath the Irish hills. It escaped once a year at Samain, bent on revenge, and none could resist its fire or the powers of its harp.

But the time came when a man found strength to make the attempt. One year, as the days drew in and autumn waned, a warrior appeared at Tara's banqueting hall, demanding audience with the King. He was a tall, well-made youth; the shield and spear he bore were fine. He was received graciously and invited to feast at the King's table. Then Cormac asked his name and business.

"I am Finn, son of Cumhal," was the young man's reply.

Then silence fell among the gathered warriors of the Fianna. The youth was indeed the very image of Cumhal, who once had been their captain, and who had been slain by one of them. Cumhal's son had been sent away for safety, and no one had seen the boy for years.

"The son of Cumhal is welcome here," said Cormac. "What is it you would have with us?"

The son of Cumhal answered, "I seek

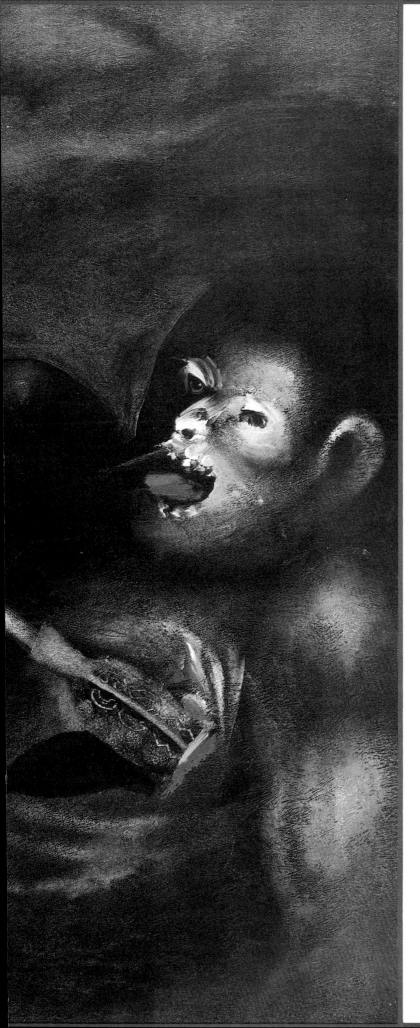

my birthright that was taken from me by the death of my father. I seek leadership of the Fianna."

The warriors around the King stirred. Some muttered at the youth's demand, but Finn's eyes turned toward them, and they were silenced.

"I will prove myself worthy," he said. "Come Samain, I will slay the shadow-man that threatens you. If I do this, King, then leadership is mine."

Cormac was silent, considering. Then he nodded. "Done," he said.

Samain came. The great gates of Tara were bolted; the warriors withdrew to the banqueting hall. Alone on the ramparts paced Finn, his footsteps sounding loud on the stones and his breath steaming in the cold air. The spear he carried, the gift of a warrior who had known his father, had a blade of bronze and rivets of gold; the blade, it was said, endowed a man with a battle fury that defeated all enemies. The spear had not been tested for long years, but it was Finn's protection against the powers of the night.

All was quiet. The roads that led from Tara stretched white in the moonlight, but Finn saw no enemy approach. Instead, harp song swelled from the trees and lingered in the air. At the sound, the young warrior paused and swayed where he stood. He leaned his head against the spear.

Then, with a great effort, he shook himself awake again: The shadow-man was upon him. It stood a full two heads taller than a human, and its form was a churning blackness that swallowed the light. Small eyes glowed red in its skull. Its mouth hung open as if to speak, but it uttered no sound. With arms of darkness, it reached to capture Finn.

The young man raised his shield and struck at the shadow with the spear. The

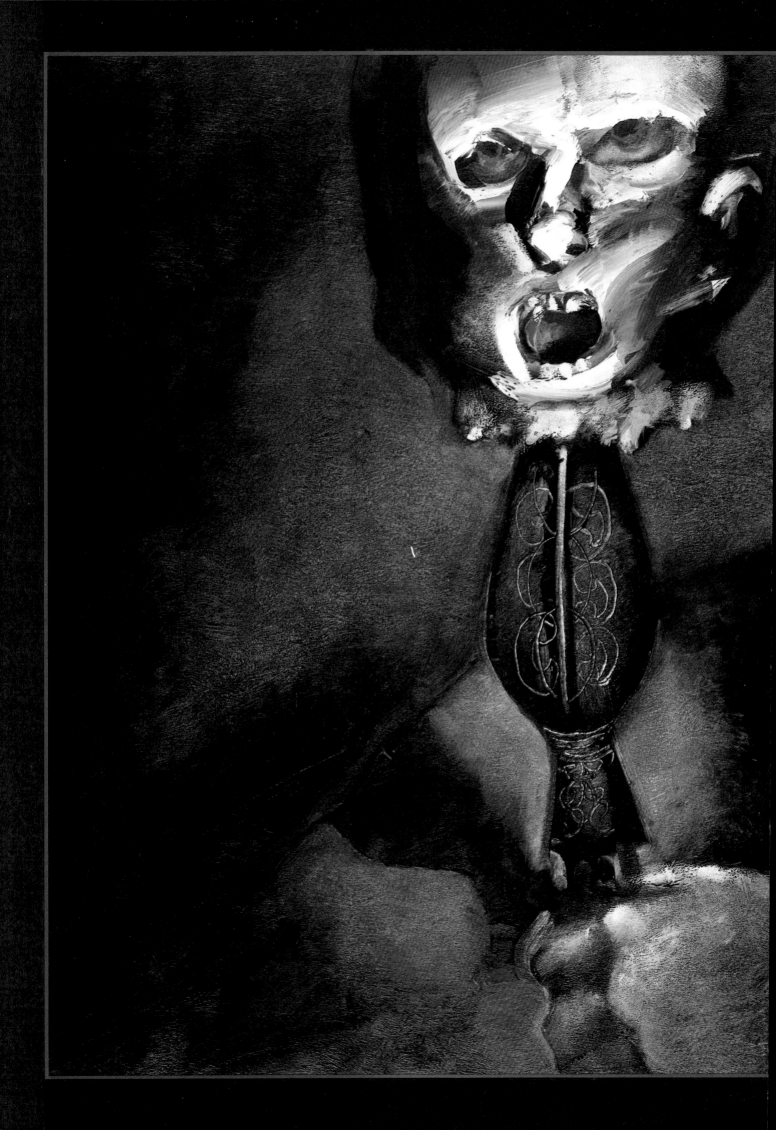

creature spat gouts of fire, which writhed around the shield and scorched the arm that bore it. Again Finn struck, and again flames leaped forth. Finn thrust once more, and this time his spear met flesh, not shadow.

In the next instant, he was alone on the ramparts. Below him, a mass of blackness lurched across the plain of Tara. The shadow creature was seeking the safety of its lair.

Caught in his battle fury, Finn lunged after the creature. Out he ran across the darkened plain, the wind raking his lungs as he chased the shadow of an elder world.

Near a swelling mound he found it crouching. He drove the spear to the creature's heart. It clawed at him and did not die. He thrust again, and then the shadow stumbled and fell, and the vapors that surrounded it swirled and faded. As the harp slipped from its grasp, it gave a wailing cry, as if to mourn the end of its power.

An hour passed. In the banqueting hall at Tara, the torches burned bright, and the warriors of the Fianna stirred once more, roused from the enchantment of the harp's melody. They awakened to a gruesome sight.

Finn stood again among them. He bore his spear high; its blade impaled a severed head, blackened and open-mouthed. Blood dripped from the neck in ragged rivulets onto the young warrior's arm, but the arm was steady. Finn threw the head to the floor at Cormac's feet.

"I have fulfilled my covenant," said Finn to the High King.

And at length, Cormac replied as he must and kept his own promise. Thus Finn, son of Cumhal, slayer of an enemy greater than any in Ireland, took his rightful place as leader of the Fianna.

Chapter Two

# W Visitations from the Realm of Shadow

When the snows of yesteryear lay across Iceland, glistening under the winter moon, a young girl arrived in Hesteyri, near the north cape of the island. She came to serve as a housemaid at a farm there. She was a brave and merry girl, and she had need of both qualities, for the farmer's land was said to be haunted. It was whispered in the neighborhood that night trolls roamed there.

Nevertheless, the girl – Gudrun by name – liked her new home. She had come from a poor hamlet, and this was a rich farm, with great grain barns and a fine stone house. Because she was just fourteen years old and an outlander, she ranked lowest among the servants. But she went about her chores in the scullery and nursery cheerfully, singing as she worked.

She did not even complain when the entire household – master and mistress, men and women servants, all of them blanketed in furs and crowded into sleighs – traveled to a neighboring farm for Evensong and feasting on Christmas Eve, leaving her alone in charge of the mistress's infant daughter. When the sleighs had faded to specks in the silvery snow fields, Gudrun closed the door and bolted it. Then she carried the baby into her mis-

tress's winter parlor and settled down by the hearth to feed the child.

It was most satisfying. The warm firelight brightened the gay colors of flower-painted storage chests and gleamed on copper pots. In a deep window embrasure, a beeswax candle shone steadily. The baby snuffled happily as it fed and at length subsided in milky contentment in its cradle. Gudrun's eyes grew heavy.

But before sleep claimed her, she was startled by a curious noise. Something – an animal, perhaps – scratched loudly along the doorsill. Then the scratching sounded around the bolt and along the lintel, higher than any animal could reach. The bolt rattled; the door strained at its frame. It did not open, however, and after a while the scratching and creaking faded away.

Gudrun gave the now-whimpering child a cloth soaked in milk to suckle. No sound came through the thick house walls, but after some moments, the candle in the window flickered. She saw the movement, and her head snapped around. A night troll's enormous face – large-pored, open-mouthed, broken-toothed – filled the frame and pressed against the glass. Its oily green eyes were fixed upon the cradle.

Gudrun looked away from the window. Hands clenched in her lap, she sat perfectly still and stared into the fire. Then she smiled grimly and, in a loud, clear voice, recited the following words:

"An iron gray with a flaxen tail, and a brass boy driving."

Child of the country that she was, Gudrun had done a clever thing. She had challenged the creature to a contest whose rules were understood and obeyed by all beings that could speak. The adversaries posed each other riddles; whoever could not answer lost the game and was placed at the mercy of the winner.

In a time when riddles are no more than children's games, it may seem strange that a life could depend on them. But in those days, when language was young and words were charged with magic, riddles — the first metaphors — were important rituals. To solve a riddle affirmed the power of the intellect over the world's mysteries. Even divine comprehension was tested this way: "Riddle reader I am called," sang Odin, the Icelanders' ancient god of wisdom and war. Among mortals, riddling contests were held at seasonal festivals, at marriages, in princely courts, and — as many a tale records — when life was threatened. The troll had no choice but to answer the human girl's challenge.

It grunted and sputtered at the window. Then, in a grating voice, with the clumsy inflections of a mouth unused to forming words, it slowly answered.

"Iron gray: needle. Flaxen tail: thread. Brass boy: thimble," it said, and made a gargling noise that might have been laughter. Now it had become the riddler.

Gudrun waited. When the troll spoke again, the words came more smoothly:

"Brothers and sisters have I none, but that man's father is my father's son."

Gudrun shrugged at the old chestnut and replied at once: "That man is the riddler's son."

Then she told another riddle, and the troll solved it and answered her in kind.

In this manner, they thrust and parried through the night. Outside, in the frozen dark, the troll shambled near the window; inside, in the firelit parlor, the girl rocked the cradle and threw logs on the hearth when the flame dwindled. Her voice grew as hoarse as the troll's, yet still she spoke on, making magic with words and forcing the troll to make magic, too.

At last, when the candle was no more than a puddle of wax and the last log had died to glowing embers, the troll posed this riddle: "Thirty white horses upon a red hill; now they champ, now they stamp, now they stand still."

Trembling with fatigue, Gudrun hesitated. Her silence lengthened. The troll gave its gargling laugh, spattering the glass with spittle. But she had the answer at last. "Your teeth and your tongue," she said, and tears filled her eyes.

The troll snarled. It moved from the window for a moment, revealing a line of scarlet along the horizon. Then Gudrun said, "On yonder hill there is a red deer. The more you shoot, the more you may; you cannot drive that deer away." The only reply was a howl and a rain of blood against the windowpane. The troll had vanished, and a shaft of morning light streamed into the room. Gudrun sank to the floor beside the hearth. "The red deer is the rising sun," she said to the baby in the cradle. The infant stared at her. Then Gudrun went to the window and peered out through the film of blood. In the snow stood a boulder that had been the troll.

Clever and courageous to the end, the young human had defeated a night haunter of the most pernicious sort—one that invaded human houses. Not all wanderers of the dark remained outside, attached to field and forest, far from the everyday paths of humankind. Many, restless and hungry, flitted from village to village and farm to farm in search of victims, and no house, however solid its timbers and snug its door, was proof against them. A knothole, a crack between stones, a hole in the roof thatch was enough of a portal for beings that could dissolve to wisps of smoke or mist in order to gain entry. The dusky corners and eaves of the dwellings provided shelter during daylight hours. And when real darkness came, when the fires were covered and good folk gone to bed, these creatures began to stir.

Silent as shadows, they stole among their human prey, now touching with bony fingers, now breathing pestilence, now whispering spells that brought foul dreams—for the powers of night were such that its offspring could harm not only human bodies but human souls as well. Disturbing dreams were the least terrible of their sendings. Death was the worst.

Children such as Gudrun and the infant she guarded were favorite victims. And it seemed that children knew this—perhaps because they had so lately emerged from the all-embracing darkness that surrounds the brief, warm light of human life. Their ears were sharper and their eyes keener than those of their elders; they could hear the faint shufflings and see the almost-imperceptible movements that betrayed the presence of danger. A draft from under the bed could mean that cruel eyes watched for small, bare feet to approach across the floorboards. Rustlings among the bedclothes could signify that something lurked there—something, perhaps, with a dark and hairy mouth and pointed teeth to bite and tear. Children were rightly wary of cupboards and stairs—spaces thick with shade. And they watched cracks in walls or ceilings or floors, sensing that a pallid hand, strong-fingered and frigid as snow, might shoot forth to lock upon ankles or snatch at nightgown hems.

Much of this was mere imagining, of course, and parents tended to dismiss such fears. Adults, after all, knew better than to believe in things that lived under the stairs or the bed or in the bedclothes; it was the eye of childhood, they said, that feared the painted devil. They called the creatures "nursery bogles" and used their names as threats to ensure good behavior.

Yet adults had their own fears. Although they rarely spoke of it, they acknowledged the reality of malevolent beings that preyed upon human young. These beings could take many forms, but the most dreaded, ironically, were human in shape. One such predator—a seeming woman—pursued her career in Scotland:

By the cold waters of the Moray Firth,

Children knew all too well the terrors of the night. One long-armed creature
of darkness laired beneath the stairs in houses, waiting for small victims.
Rawhead-and-Bloody-Bones was the name the youngsters gave it.

on a peninsula called the Black Isle, stood the small fishing village of Cromarty, whose infants were always at risk. The men who went to sea in search of herring knew this; so did the village wives, but all were helpless to thwart the force that ruled the dark.

The haunter was particularly sinister because she had something of the mother in her. Up and down the lanes of the little town she wandered, her feet silent on the cobblestones. Those who caught a glimpse of her said that she wore green, like some ancient tree spirit, and that she bore in her arms a sickly, wrinkled demon child with fiery eyes and sharp-pointed little fingers.

At a cottage where a human baby dwelled, she would wait, huddled out of sight, until the household slept. Then she would lift the latch and glide in. As she stooped to the cradle, there would be no more sound than a tiny whimper. Then the woman in green would go to the hearth and by the glow of smoldering coals bathe her own infant's withered skin. It was the image of maternal caring, except that she bathed the creature in warm blood, drawn from the human child. That child's eyes would never open again.

No one could explain where she came from or why, mercifully, her visitations at last ceased. And no one knew how many little ones were laid in rough pine coffins by her doing. Infant deaths, swift and mysterious, were common then. Churchyards all across Europe bore sad and silent witness to the fragility of young life. The ground was thick with the graves of children. A man and woman who bore a dozen babies were lucky to see half survive the birthing and live past the age of five. Disease killed them; starvation killed them; and, said parents, so did creatures of the Scottish nightwalker's kind.

Babies in Bulgaria were likely to be visited in the night by a hag whose head was that of an ox. This thing would crawl into cottages and raise itself enough to see into the cradles; when it did so, its foul breath spread over the tiny bodies, bringing pestilence. Children thus visited wasted for a day or two, then were gone.

The woods and fields of nearby Poland, Czechoslovakia and Russia were haunted by a similar creature — the *nočnitsa*, or "night hag" — said to torment infants whose mothers had neglected to bless them at bedtime. This creature tickled the tiny feet, or prodded the little bellies, or — worse still — sucked blood from fine veins, all for the pleasure of hearing the children cry. The night hag vanished if an adult entered the room, but it left its marks behind; the *nočnitsa* was a bringer of fever and disease.

Such assaults on children were terrible: It was a perversion of nature that the young should die before their parents' lives had run their courses. Yet the dark was fraught with danger for adults as well as children, and for rich and poor alike. The lord and his lady in their tapestry-hung bed were warmer but not safer than the villein and his family, huddled together on pallets of straw under coverings of deerskin. All of them, caught in the web of sleep, were as helpless as infants then.

Sleep was an intimidating mystery. Ev-

No lock or bolt was proof against night prowlers, as Scottish folk knew. Through
their sleeping villages crept a green-clad figure with a wizened child. As easily
as moonlight, she slipped into their houses, seeking the balm of infants' blood.

ery man and woman who looked upon a sleeping companion knew the fleeting loneliness of seeing the beloved and familiar face become remote and expressionless, locked away in the solitude that is the human lot. Everyone knew the pang of tenderness at seeing the sleeper, alert by day, sink into an unwatchfulness as vulnerable as a child's. The sleeper's stillness seemed a little death, and indeed, people named sleep "death's brother."

Yet it was not death: As every man and woman understood, a vital life flourished within sleep, a second self that was released in rest. In leaving the world of the everyday, the sleeper entered the realm of dreams. Within the motionless body, a cloud of images danced and played—magic shadow shapes that came and went like the wind. Freed from the bonds of dailiness, the soul soared. As the Greek physician Hippocrates once said, "When the body sleeps, the spirit wakes."

And how did it wake and where did it go? What sent the sleeper on his enigmatic journey? People had many beliefs about this, not all of them frightening. Children said that dreams came from the Sand Man, a sprite dressed in bright-colored silks, who sprinkled dust on their eyes to make pictures in their heads. French children thought the dream-giver was a woman called La Dormette. Their elders, however, said that, freed from the prison of flesh and bone, the spirit left the body.

In Serbia, wise folk believed that every night, the spirits of the sleeping populace—and of their dogs and cats and cattle—sailed out cottage windows and chimneys and keyholes. Light as air, they soared high above the treetops and church spires, flying to lonely mountaintops. There, these spirits, called *zduhaczs* by the Serbs, engaged in furious battles with one another. The victors brought health and bountiful harvests to the sleepers whose souls they were. If a *zduhacz* perished in battle, however, its mortal body would never again awaken to the light of day.

More commonly, it was thought that the dreamer's soul left the body visibly—as a vapor, perhaps, or as a butterfly or singing bird. In this guise, the soul went wandering, and its adventures were recalled as dreams, many of which came to be told as tales. One of the earliest was that of Guntram, a Sixth Century Frankish King.

Guntram ruled a small territory in the mountains of the Lower Rhine, a kingdom carved out after the dissolution of the Roman Empire. His story began on a summer day during a hunt in his own forests. Made drowsy by the heat, he lay down in the shade near a brook to rest, leaving one of his warriors to stand guard.

The warrior reported later that he had paced for some moments among the trees near the sleeping King and at last came to a halt. His eye was attracted by a movement near Guntram's face: A tiny, jewel-like serpent had appeared there. With raised head and flicking tongue, it surveyed the ground; then, in the graceful, undulating fashion of its species, it made its way through the grass toward the brook.

At the bank among the water reeds, it paused, head swaying back and forth. The guard, amused by the creature's apparent perplexity, laid his sword over the water as a bridge. At once (continued on page 51)

# Battling the Spider-Demon

Even the bravest of mortals quailed before the wrath of night goblins, as shown by a tale of ancient Japan. In that country there lived a nobleman named Raiko, who boldly undertook to rid the city of Kyoto of its demons. Retaliation by the fiends of darkness was swift. A wasting fever struck the hero. For many days and nights he lay in his chamber, guarded by companions but assailed by sick fancies. And on a night aswarm with dreams, the visions gathered solid form. Raiko awoke and found himself chained to his pallet by countless silken filaments. Above him waved many-jointed, bristling

legs. Huge eyes glittered. Raiko had become a spider's prey.

No sound came from Raiko's companions; they sat against the wall entranced, neither watching nor speaking. How long Raiko lay helpless in the spider's trap, he never afterward could tell. Nor could he tell how he found strength to grasp the sword that lay beside him. But grasp it he did. He cut his silken bonds and swung the weapon so that it slashed into the hairy legs. From the spider's maw came a gurgling scream, but the warrior could fight no more. He fell back, trembling with weakness, and closed his eyes and waited for death.

Death did not come. The wounded spider, leaving Raiko

where he lay, scuttled through the shadows to the safety of its earthen lair. Its departure lifted the web of spells that had held Raiko's companions. Awaking, they looked in horror upon their prostrate general and the sword that had fallen from his fingers; then they saw the twitching spider legs beside him and the trail of malodorous blood that led into the dark. Determined upon revenge, they followed the track to its end and slew the maimed monster. And when they returned, they were overjoyed to find Raiko alive and well. Ever after his sword was called Kumokiri, or "Spider cutter," for its work against the demon of the night.

the little snake slithered across, continuing up a rise on the far bank to the safety of a bracken-bordered hole it found there.

After some moments, the emerald head reappeared, and the serpent made its journey in reverse, sliding down the bank, across the sword and then, so swiftly that the guard had no time to stop it, into the mouth of the sleeping King.

Apparently unharmed, Guntram stirred and woke. He sat up, leaned against a linden tree and, with a smile, told the guard of the dream he had had. He had traveled alone, said Guntram, through a desert of towering reedlike trees, until he had arrived at a broad river. While he contemplated the waters, wondering how to get to the other side, an iron bridge had swung down from the sky; this he had crossed. It led him to a mountain cave in which he had found a giant's treasure: disks of silver piled as high as castle walls; massive chains hung with boulders of ruby; hoops as large as chariot wheels, engraved with stiff, dancing figures.

The guard stared at Guntram in baffled silence for some moments. Finally he told the King of the little serpent's odyssey from mouth to hole and back again. Together, then, the two men stepped across the narrow brook and dug among the bracken where the guard had seen the snake disappear.

In the earth they found treasure, the booty of some forgotten lord. There were piles of coins, ruby-studded necklaces, armbands decorated with ancient festal scenes. The treasure was the one that Guntram's spirit had seen with serpent's eyes, although shrunk to proper proportions.

Or so the old tale said. Such stories gave rise to the belief that small animals should not be harmed: Perhaps they embodied the souls of sleepers who would not awake again if the animals were killed. And because of these tales, people said that sleeping men and women should be wakened gradually, so that their souls would have time to return to their bodies. Otherwise, the sleepers would die.

Such calamities were rare, however. Most dreamers drifted undisturbed through their nightly ventures, rejoining their bodies in good time to assure a safe awakening. The wisps of dreams that remained in memory might be recalled with curiosity, for dreams were long believed to be portents of the future – so much so that from earliest times, wise men and women kept books describing the fates nocturnal visions foreshadowed (*page 62*).

But a dream could be something other than a portent or the wanderings of the sleeper's soul. People believed that the night loosed a host of powerful creatures more corporeal than dreams and more subtle and elusive than trolls, creatures whose only purpose was to exhaust and corrupt and kill mortals. They leaped upon the sleeper's breast, crushing out human strength and will, and bringing with them terrible dreams. In England such a creature was called a nightmare, in France *cauchemar*, in Germany *Mahr*, in Lithuania *mara*, all of them names deriving from the same source as the Anglo-Saxon *mara*, meaning "crusher." The Latin term was *incubus*, which carried a similar meaning. Greeks

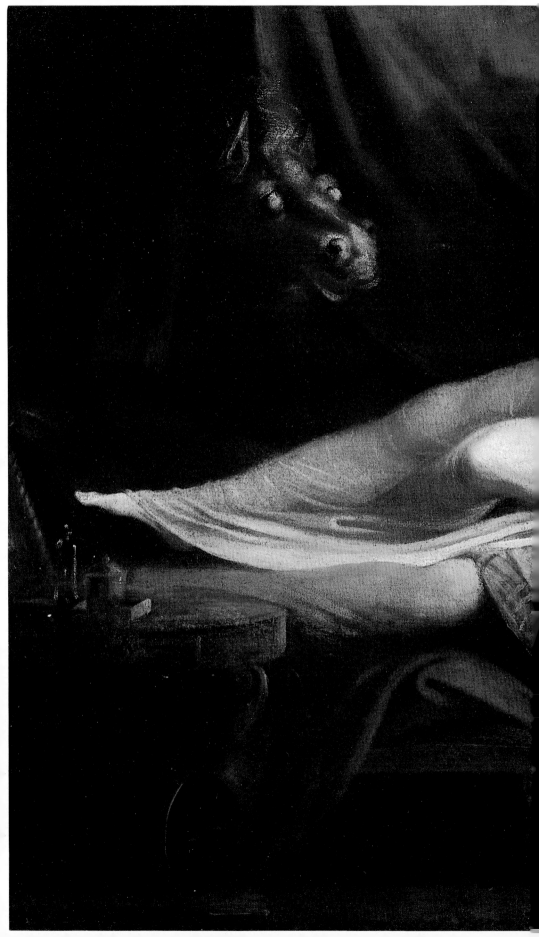

With talons that caught and remorselessly held, with weight that crushed the breath away,
    with eyes that gleamed foul images, shadow demons invaded human houses and human dreams.

*An implacable despoiler and an enemy of humankind from the beginning of time, Lilith the seducer slid into men's dreams, stealing her victims' vigor and shattering their spirits.*

called the spirit *ephialtes*—or the "leaper."

In every land, such beings were feared. To prevent their entry into sleeping chambers and to keep the terror away, country-folk tried age-old remedies. Some never slept with their heads to the north, where lay the land of death and darkness. Some placed their shoes by their beds with the pointed toes facing outward; it was hoped that this small show of sharpness would repel intruders. Some laid a coffin nail under the foot of the bed: Iron was thought inimical to the beings of the other world.

These precautions were frail barriers against the demons of the dark, hungry as those demons were for human souls. Seducers and defilers, they debased the most innocent, sapping human vigor and leaving behind exhausted shells.

The mother of this malign company was Lilith, a daughter of the eldest world. Hebrew tales told how she was born of dust to be the mate of the first father, Adam; how, rotten with haughtiness, she left his garden in a fury, vowing eternal vengeance on him and on his descendants. Coldly beautiful, infinitely seductive, she survived the centuries, and her very name seemed to whisper *laylah*, the Hebrew word for "night." But Lilith was a hater of men and a slayer of children. She sought to replace human infants with her own foul brood. No Jewish household was safe from her ravages, for Lilith followed the paths of the exiles to the farthest corners of the earth. In the dark hours, she stole into nurseries, strangling newborns where they lay. Then she glided through the hallways to chambers where the young men slept. For all the shame and fear of it, none could resist the pleasures she offered, and so Lilith got the children she desired.

Her daughters were a vast brood, nightmares all, who haunted the earth for generations. They were shadow lovers, eaters of souls, and they drew the men they captured far from the world of humankind. Such was the nightmare's power that the men she visited faded until they were as tenebrous as she. They spurned the day and lost the strength to love.

In Norway, a nightmare spirit could enter a house in the soft shape of a cat, if she wished, or take the form of vapor and float in through a chink in the wall. She could be caught and brought into daylight by the men she seduced, but traffic with her was full of subtle dangers, as a Norwegian story tells.

The tale begins with the dreams of a fisherman who worked on the gray waters of the northern coast. He was a young man, vigorous and red-cheeked from days in the cold salt air, but the time came when his eyes grew dull and his hands trembled. He lived alone and made no one welcome in his cottage. Something had begun to haunt it, and night after night he dreamed of things he could not tell by day.

One night, resisting sleep with all his

will, he met his tormentor. The hours passed silently, save for the creaking of the house and the rattle of the windows as the north wind beat against them. He lay without a light, but even in the darkness, he saw the fingers of mist that drifted in from a crack in the stone wall beside his bed. Luminous and curling, the vapor lay on the air; with delicate tendrils, it searched among the bedclothes.

The fisherman leaped into action. He flung himself from the bed and slapped his hand over the crack through which the mist had entered. It was easy to plug the crack with fat from his lamp, easy to light the lamp with a spill flamed at the hearth. When the little light steadied, he peered at the place where the mist had been.

But it was gone. In its place a woman stood, and she was no ruddy village maid. Her flesh was so pale it seemed translucent; her hair was a cloud of darkness, and she gazed at him with liquid, knowing eyes. The fisherman put out the light.

In the morning she still lay beside him, unsleeping and watchful, trapped by daylight. He told her roughly that since she had chosen to haunt him, she could serve him as a wife: She was pretty, he said, and she gave him pleasure. She could set to the work that other wives did.

The woman obeyed silently, without demur, and the tasks he assigned were admirably performed. She cooked and mended the nets. With her white hands, she hung his catch of mackerel and herring over smoking, seaweed-lined pits to dry.

His neighbors asked the fisherman where he had gotten his obedient wife, but he rebuffed such questions sharply, and soon the matter was mentioned no more. Still, people did not fail to notice how the pale woman grew rosy and strong. They saw the small smile that trembled on her red lips when her eyes rested on the fisherman. As for him, each day he grew more sullen and withdrawn. He seemed to fade: His face paled to dull gray, marked by the hectic glitter of his eyes.

During the sunless winter hours, no windows glowed in the cottage. Inside, by the dim firelight, the fisherman each night surveyed his prisoner and said, "Tell me what you are and where you came from."

But she was the stronger at night. She smiled a secret smile at him and invariably replied, "I do not know." Then she beckoned, and helplessly he obeyed.

The fisherman became wraithlike; he took to drink and to staring at his blooming captive with hate-filled eyes. Always, he asked his nightly question: "Tell me what you are and where you came from."

"I do not know."

Anger saved the fisherman. One night, when he had drunkenly asked his question and received his answer, he ignored the beckoning hand. Instead, he stumbled to the wall and, with clumsy fingers, picked at the hardened fat that sealed the chink beside the bed. When he felt the night air, he turned to the woman and mumbled thickly, "You entered by this portal, lady. Leave by it."

The woman trembled; her pale flesh wavered and dissolved into vapor. Ribbons of the mist streamed upward and, light as a sigh, out the chink in the wall. The last the

*The dream lover called the mara was a thief cloaked in darkness. Taking vapor form, she slipped into sleeping chambers through tiny chinks and crevices, then assumed the shape of a woman to claim the souls of men.*

It was dangerous to weep too long for the dead. The demon lover of one maiden answered her mournful cries and carried her to an earthen marriage bed.

fisherman heard of his nightmare was a single, drifting, mournful wail that might have been the winter wind.

The fisherman was lucky. Made miserable by a plague of dreams, he had trapped the nightmare, not understanding that no mortal strength matched the hunger of a daughter of darkness. He had held the creature in his arms and then, even as his death was brought near by so doing, had pulled free of her killing charms because of the drink-induced confusion of his senses.

Not many shared his fortune; the eaters of souls were too strong. And their powers increased when, rather than arriving randomly, they came in answer to a summons. No one would ever issue such a summons intentionally, of course. But in those days, the door of darkness was sometimes opened inadvertently.

What turned the key was human grief. Bereaved men and women who mourned excessively and called upon their loved ones were apt to get an answer that put them at the gravest risk: In those days, words were so strong that they could bring murderous spirits into being.

Such was the case in Hungary, where naming of the dead called forth demon lovers. The tales were much the same: A widow, perhaps, would mourn her husband and wish for even an hour with him again. That night, a bright star trailing sparkling fire would arc across the blackness, as if the fabric of heaven were being rent. A man would appear before the widow, the very image of her dead husband.

He was, however, no husband but a semblance, a seeming man inhabited by a demon's spirit. Then and during the nights that followed, he would secretly tryst with her. In spite of her nocturnal joys, she would wither and fade until at last, if she did not discover the truth about her visitor, she would die and join the company of darkness. What killed her was a *lidérc*, a spirit that fed on her love and pain. Only by recognizing the spirit for what it was could she avert such a fate. The means of recognition was a grotesque anomaly — hard to see in the dark — which indicated that her bed was shared not by her husband but by a *lidérc:* One of its feet would be shaped like that of a goose.

Other beings of the *lidérc's* kind haunted Europe, and not all of them acted so slowly and insidiously: Some moved swiftly to the kill. A Prussian tale of such a spirit centered on a maiden named Lenore, who lived in the chill flatlands that bordered the Baltic Sea. The men of her village — all but the grandfathers and little boys — were impressed into the army of the Prussian King, as often happened in those days. Among them was her own lover. Under the eye of the King's officers, the company marched briskly south to fight, and nothing was seen of them for many months.

Lenore waited patiently as the slow days dawned, darkened, and dawned again. She watched the highway that led into the village, and so she knew when the soldiers began to return. She saw the menfolk of her sisters and her cousins, some of them blinded, some missing arms or legs, all of them ragged and joyful to be home. Her lover never appeared.

He had died on a battlefield far away, but no word came of his fate. At length, Lenore shut herself in her chamber and paced alone, dry-eyed, hearing nothing and saying not a word. In the night, however, when the town slept, she wept and whispered her grief to the darkness. She called upon her lover to return. She asked for death, to give her heart ease.

Death would not come, only one long night to face and then the next. But at last one winter evening, when the town lay locked in sleep, horseshoes clattered on the cobblestones of the street. They halted by her house, and she heard her lover's voice. He called her name. In the hall below, a door swung open. His familiar footstep sounded on the stair, and Lenore was there at once to greet him.

He did not smile, nor did he hold out his arms. He stood stiffly on the stair, his face expressionless. His voice, when he spoke, was that of a soldier giving orders.

"Come ride with me now," he said. "I will take you to our marriage bed."

Worn and unthinking from nights of weeping, Lenore obeyed. Just as she was, wearing only her nightshift, she descended the shadowy stair and followed her lover out the door. Without protest she mounted behind him and wrapped her arms around his waist. The horse flew through the village street and out onto the broad highway, where a winter landscape spread silver before her.

Shivering with the cold, she held fast to her lover, but no warmth came from him, and he did not speak. A rank, sweet smell enveloped her. On either side of the path the gaunt black branches of the trees reached out, waving blindly in the moonlight. Among them, above the thunder of the horse's hoofs, she heard the reedy wail of an owl's cry.

She called her lover's name, and he spoke once, over his shoulder, so that the wind caught his words, but all he said was, "We ride swiftly, as we must, to reach the place before the cock crow."

And, indeed, they rode as swiftly as the wind, so that rooftops, tree branches and fields flashed by in blurs.

They slowed at last, after hours of riding, in unfamiliar country, bleak and bare. An iron gate swung open before them, and the horse cantered into a churchyard.

It was not empty. Black-robed figures crowded around the horse, plucking with cold hands at Lenore's shift and tugging at her arms. They pulled her from the horse, and her lover slid to the ground beside her. His uniform was a rotted shroud; his dry-flesh face stretched into a wintry grin.

"This is the wedding party," he said. "There is our wedding bed." He pointed to her feet, where the earth yawned open.

The end of the tale was told by the church sexton, who arose at dawn to tend the graves. In the churchyard he found the exhausted horse and smelled the stench of death. He saw the mound of a freshly filled grave, where no grave had been before. On the tumbled earth lay a scrap of lace. The sexton made no move to touch it. Graveyard scavenging stirred up demons and other angry spirits, and soon another night would fall, setting them free to roam among mortals once more.

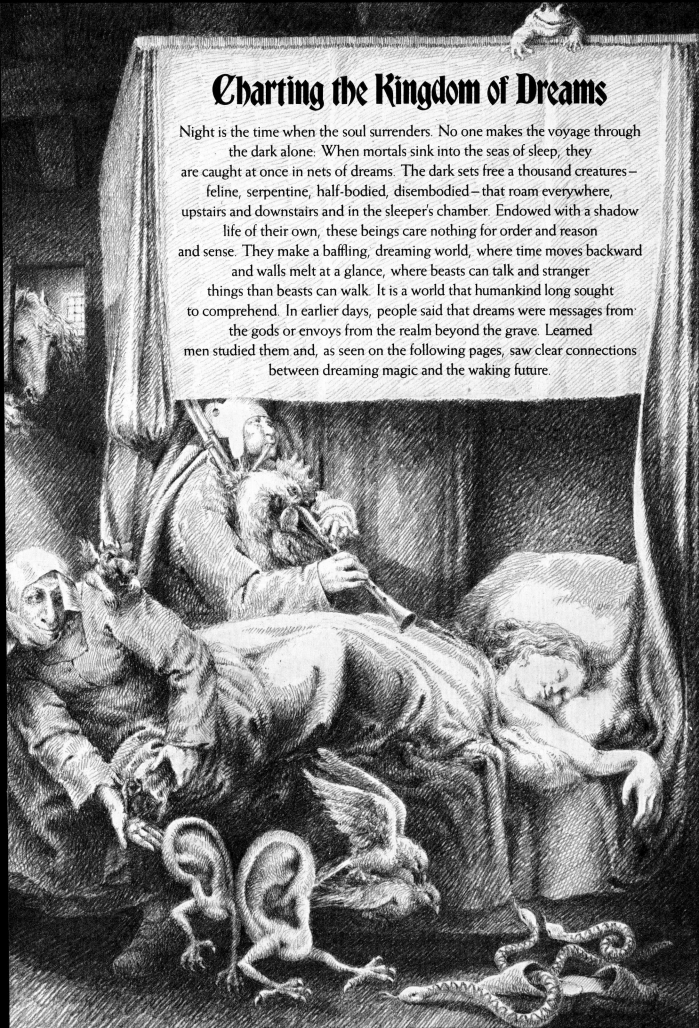

# Charting the Kingdom of Dreams

Night is the time when the soul surrenders. No one makes the voyage through the dark alone: When mortals sink into the seas of sleep, they are caught at once in nets of dreams. The dark sets free a thousand creatures — feline, serpentine, half-bodied, disembodied — that roam everywhere, upstairs and downstairs and in the sleeper's chamber. Endowed with a shadow life of their own, these beings care nothing for order and reason and sense. They make a baffling, dreaming world, where time moves backward and walls melt at a glance, where beasts can talk and stranger things than beasts can walk. It is a world that humankind long sought to comprehend. In earlier days, people said that dreams were messages from the gods or envoys from the realm beyond the grave. Learned men studied them and, as seen on the following pages, saw clear connections between dreaming magic and the waking future.

A dream of flight, by wind or wing, was said to be a sign that the dreamer would soon enjoy some great success.

And what of dream pursuits by shadow-men through alien streets? They meant turbulence and trouble by daylight.

Scholars said that if the dreamer sank into watery depths, his waking fate was to be drawn down into poverty.

Fortunetellers heard of dreams of leafy stillness, of warm flesh drying and limbs twisting into bark and branch, and said,

that these dreams meant impending illness.

# Chapter Three

# Blood Feasts of the Damned

One long-distant summer when nightingales sang through the evenings in the gardens of Baghdad and the air was heavy with the scent of roses, a merchant of that city grew mistrustful of the wife he loved and took a path that led him into the heart of darkness. This is his tale:

He was called Abul-Hassan, she Nadilla. He was rich and powerful, she the daughter of an elderly scholar whose dark little house lay huddled in the poor quarter of the city. But when he first saw her in the spring of that year, her beauty wove a spell about him. Soon thereafter, he took Nadilla from her timid parent and made her his wife.

The house he brought her to had many rooms and courtyards, but Nadilla seemed to care little for it. She drifted apathetically through the lengthening summer days, staying always in the cool shadows of the house, away from the sun that glared on the white walls outside and flickered among the palm fronds. She ate almost nothing. Lost in some unfathomable reverie, she ignored the servants. Indeed, she appeared hardly to see her husband.

But when daylight faded and the lamps were lighted, Nadilla brightened. The stirring evening breeze seemed to revive her,

and she became the wife Abul-Hassan desired, glowing and tender. With playful ease, she enticed him early to bed each night. Abul-Hassan noted the alteration but put his wife's daytime listlessness down to the dust-laden heat. The coming of cool weather would restore her, he felt sure. His sleep each night was deep and dreamless.

A night came, however, when Abul-Hassan awakened suddenly in the dark. His wife was no longer beside him, and there was no sign of her in the room. He lay alert for some moments, but finally the soft patter of palm branches moving outside the window drew him back into the embrace of sleep.

He awakened again only when the liquid wails of the muezzins echoed over the town from minaret to minaret, calling the faithful to dawn prayer. Nadilla had just returned. He watched from under his lashes while she removed cloak and veil, and when she slipped into his bed, he lay as though asleep.

The next night she disappeared again. The third night he followed her.

Out through the gardens and into the moonlit city she ran lightly, as though to meet a lover, and Abul-Hassan pursued.

She made her way down twisting streets and along the now-quiet alleyways of the bazaar, finally halting at the gate of a walled house in the oldest quarter of the town. The gate before her seemed to spring open of its own accord.

Clinging to shadows for secrecy, Abul-Hassan followed his wife into a courtyard, down a winding stone stair and into a corridor. There he paused, appalled at the sacrilege of entering such a place. The walls were lined with sarcophagi. This was a family tomb.

He went on slowly, guided by the faint jingling of the silver bangles Nadilla wore on her ankles and the whisper of her silken trousers. Before long, he came upon an archway. The jingling had stopped, and so he peered around it cautiously.

Beyond lay a stone crypt, faintly lighted by a funerary lamp set in a niche in the wall, and close by the crypt, amid a pathetic jumble of bones and grave offerings, knelt his wife. When Abul-Hassan saw what she was doing, his heart lurched.

Panting and whimpering, Nadilla dragged a body from its coffin. She pulled an arm free. Then, with a high-pitched snarl, she bent her head and tore at the gray flesh with sharp little teeth.

Abul-Hassan waited to see no more of the horror. He fled to his house. During that long night he lay tormented by bleak and turbulent thoughts. His wife slipped into his bed again at dawn, heavy-eyed and flushed. He said nothing to her, but all through the next day, he watched her narrowly. She was no different from what she had been before—vague, languid, clinging to shadows and brightening when they lengthened and dusk returned. Abul-Hassan offered her food then. She refused it, but she smiled at him, and when he saw the white teeth flash, he could contain himself no longer.

"Perhaps we should find you dead men's flesh, Wife," he said.

She stiffened. Her eyes began to glitter blindly, and her lips stretched wide in a mindless grin, cruelly distorting her pretty face. Then, nimble as a cat, she sprang.

Abul-Hassan was ready for her. With his curved knife, he stabbed his wife to death. He buried her at once, without ceremony, outside his walls so that his house would not be defiled. If the servants noticed his activities, they made no comment. Abul-Hassan was a stern master, and the strange and silent woman he had brought into the house to be his wife had found no favor with them.

The trials of Abul-Hassan were not ended, however. He discovered this the third night after the killing. As he tossed and turned, staring out the window at the stars that winked between the palm fronds, his wife—or some ghastly simulacrum of his wife—came to him.

She rose near the foot of the bed, from among the carpets and pillows on the floor. Her white shift clung to her in blood-crusted patches where he had stabbed her; one arm hung stiffly at her side; her face was masklike, the lips loose and the eyes sunken. Whatever animated her was not life. She moved with the jerking awkwardness of a marionette, and a foul, necrotic stench veiled her.

In a grim parody of wifely affection, she climbed onto the bed where Abul-Hassan lay transfixed and crawled leadenly over him, wheezing and mumbling as she moved. The nauseating stench grew stronger, the tortured wheezing louder. She bent her head, and her sharp teeth neared the tendons of his neck.

Abul-Hassan threw the creature off and leaped from the bed, shouting for the servants and for a light. Within moments, the room was crowded with people, and the thing that had materialized from the night was gone.

But Abul-Hassan surmised the truth of this creature's origin. Nadilla had allied herself to evil during life. She had been human, but barely so—flinching from the day, flourishing in the dark, and growing ever more addicted to human flesh. After death, some nameless force of darkness had claimed her wholly, using her to satisfy its own craving. She had become a vampire, a soulless corpse that drew its sustenance from human blood.

Abul-Hassan went to Nadilla's father and forced him to tell what he knew. The old man confessed that his daughter had been a witch who sold her soul to Satan and thereafter lived a life of secret vice. Such was her power that during life she had bound even her own parent to silence and fear.

Together, then, father and husband dug up the body and burned it to ashes, so that there would be nothing left to walk in the night, when good folk slept. Abul-Hassan cast the ashes into the Tigris River to flow southward to the Persian Gulf and disperse in the great sea that bathes the edges of the earth.

Nadilla never troubled the living again, but she was one of a vast and ghostly company that trod the world in days gone by, and her companions in darkness pursued their secret way long after she had vanished. These creatures struck terror in human hearts: They existed in defiance of every natural rule.

In the natural order of things, life was a one-way journey: The living progressed inexorably from cradle to grave, and once the earth covered them, they were gone forever. Their souls soared free to a destination no one knew; their bodies, abandoned, crumbled quietly to dust.

Yet sometimes the natural order went awry, and the earth refused its duty. The buried corpse — now empty, putrefying flesh — rose up as a vampire. Because it had no soul, such a creature showed no reflection in a mirror and cast no shadow on a wall: Both reflections and shadows, it was said, were images of the human spirit.

Shadowless though they were, vampires had cunning, strength and an inexorable will. No grave could keep a vampire in, and no house could keep one out. Scratching patiently within its tomb, it could dig itself a passageway to the air, through which it drifted, wraithlike, to the surface of the earth to begin its hunt. If necessary in its search for victims, the vampire could pass through a keyhole or a crack in a wall. To reach its hapless prey unnoticed, it could change its shape and fly like an owl or prowl like a cat.

What were these creatures that sought

*Eluding the grasp of the grave, the undead rose each night to seek the sustenance of blood. Thus the fathomless hunger of the creature Nadilla drove her to attack her husband—a cruel betrayal of life and love.*

the blood of living men and women? No one could tell. Bloodthirsty spirits had haunted the earth since the very beginning of time—not vampires but their predecessors in evil. Ancient Babylon, for instance, was plagued by the *ekimmu*, a dead soul that coveted human flesh and blood. Among the Jews of the ancient world, the myriad demon offspring of Lilith—the nightmare queen—sucked the veins of mortal children.

True vampires were human corpses that had been invaded by blood-hungry spirits. The mortal body was merely a vehicle for the spirit, which itself had no shape and no means of satisfying its appetite. Some corpses suited the spirit's purposes better than others. Those most susceptible to invasion were the bodies of men and women who, like Nadilla, had given themselves over to evil during their lives.

Existence as a vampire was thus a form of damnation. For example, the most famous of vampires, Rumania's Count Dracula (the name meant "dragon" or "devil") was thought to be the enlivened corpse of a petty ruler whose savage practice of spitting his enemies earned him the epithet "Vlad the Impaler."

Among the host of the damned were men and women who had been executed as criminals or who had committed suicide, the ultimate sin against heaven. The bodies of both were to be found at crossroads: the criminals swinging from gibbets, stiff-legged and raven-pecked, rotting in the wind, and the suicides in shallow graves under the earth. It was thought that if such

corpses should be animated once again, the divergence of roads would confuse the malevolent spirits that inhabited them and so keep the bodies bound in place.

Other conditions besides an evil life put the dead at risk, it was said. In Greece, for instance, the living could be cursed so that when they died they could not rest; their corpses would be prey to hideous invasion. A person under such a curse might be shunned, as though he already partook of the baleful nature that would animate him after death.

So great was the fear of vampires, in fact, that any deviation from the norm in living people was considered to be a sign of susceptibility to vampirism. Among those thought to be likely victims were illegitimate children born of illegitimate parents, seventh sons or seventh daughters, children born with birthmarks, with teeth or with harelips, and children born with cauls—membranes that covered their heads. It was said that children born of mothers who had been gazed upon by vampires during their pregnancies—especially during the last three months of the pregnancies—were doomed to the vampire state.

Children born on Christmas Day were considered vulnerable, as were children who died unbaptized, or indeed, any person who died in a state of sin, without the blessing of the Church. In Slavic countries, where most people were dark-haired and dark-eyed, it was thought that blue-eyed redheads would become vampires after death. In Bulgaria, the condition was said to run in families. It was also assumed that those who were

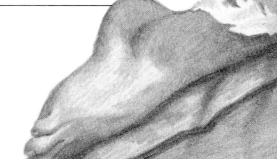

attacked by vampires would die to rise up again as bloodsuckers themselves.

The fear of the horror was far more pervasive than the horror itself. It showed in the anxious rituals surrounding death, which served not only to keep the mortal shell of the beloved safe from harm, but also to prevent it from harming others.

These funerary rituals began at the very hour of death, for the body was thought most vulnerable to lurking spirits in the period before burial. The body was tenderly laid out, often in a room barricaded at door and window with brambles, which prevented the entry of wandering spirits and also of animals — especially cats — that might house those spirits. It was thought that if a cat jumped over the sleeping dead, the dead would surely walk again.

This fear of spirits led to the custom of watching beside the body before it was buried: The watchers were, in reality, guardians of the helpless dead. In Ireland, the watching evolved into the riotous Irish wake; in Russia, the deathwatch was formalized to the point where mourners followed the bier to church and stayed beside it throughout the night, intoning psalms as protection against the dark. During the night hours, the mourners knew, the dead might move in their coffins, rustling their winding sheets and scratching at the coffin lids, seeking the means to leave their wooden prisons. It was even said that Russian peasants took barnyard cocks with them into the church to help keep the vigil. If the corpse they watched should stir, the birds could be pinched to make them crow, thereby fooling the dead into thinking that dawn had come: Vampires were powerless by daylight.

The same care prevailed in conveying the body to its tomb, and in many countries, extra measures were taken to protect the living. In Russia, for instance, mourners following a bier often wore masks to prevent the dead from recognizing them. Funeral processions left the burying grounds by twisting, devious routes, so that even if the corpse should rise again, it would not find its former fellows.

The rituals of death were particularly elaborate in Greece, where a man might be sent to his grave with an angry imprecation that denied him his rightful rest, and where vendettas between island families led to centuries of blood guilt, revenge and terrifying hauntings by murder victims. Fear of the murdered dead, in fact, resulted in the hideous mutilations Greek murderers once practiced on their victims: They cut off the hands and feet and placed them in the corpse's armpits or tied them with bands to its breast, to keep the wakeful dead eternally crippled.

Greek funeral customs, by contrast, were designed not to shackle the dead but to ease their passage and protect their remains. Garlanded with olive leaves and accompanied by crowds of wailing mourners, the body was carried to its last bed. All along the way, the ground was watered from earthenware urns, which then were shattered so that they could not be used by the living again.

The grave itself was richly supplied with clothing and with food — honey cakes and

Because those who had done evil during their lives might do evil after death, measures were taken to thwart their return. Criminals were hanged at distant crossroads so that their revenants would have difficulty finding the way back home.

rice, dishes of boiled wheat adorned with flowers and ribbons—to ensure the comfort of the dead. And at the last, the body was given extra safety in the form of a coin placed in the silent mouth. This was not, as often thought, the famous "Charon's obol," or money to pay the ferryman who transported souls to hell; it was a charm that barred demonic spirits from entering the dead body through the mouth and giving it spurious life.

Thus protected, the dead were consigned to rest, and wine was poured over the earth that covered them. A light—called an "unsleeping lamp" because it never failed—was often left burning for three years beside the grave, that being the time it took the flesh to rot away to harmless dust. If all went well and no vampire walked, the family dug up its dead after three years of interment, washed the flesh-less bones in wine and returned them to their earthen bed.

That was the best that could be hoped for the dead—quiet and peaceful fading in the dark. The worst was that the body would not dissolve, that lying in its grave would be not clean white bones but a soot-colored, shiny-skinned, swollen and incorrupt body bearing a close resemblance to its living predecessor but filled with a life that was not its own. This was the Greek vampire, "inflated like drums and black for a thousand years." It was called a *vrykolakas*, meaning "drumlike," and the grotesquely distended corpse in fact gave forth a hollow booming when struck.

The earliest *vrykolakes* were terrifying but not inevitably evil. They seemed to possess no appetite for human blood: They were simply revenants, imprisoned halfway between life and death because of some earthly matter left unsettled at burial. It was even said that some crept back

*The hours and days after death were perilous. If a body was not carefully guarded from wandering spirits, it might become a host for evil and burst the bonds of its coffin.*

to their old homes at night to mend their children's shoes, cut wood, draw water from the well, and plow fields that might otherwise lie fallow.

Most *vrykolakes* came for darker, sadder reasons. They might be instruments of revenge, seeking redress for wrongs done them or their families. These situations gave rise to the oft-told tales of jealous husbands who in life discovered that their faithless wives had taken lovers. It might happen that such husbands died before they could deal with the perfidy and avenge their stained honor. Then their corpses had no rest: Night after night their distorted shapes would appear in their widows' chambers, plaguing the women unmercifully. Indeed, the vampire's tendency to haunt his own home and loved ones was so pronounced that it gave rise to the rustic Greek proverb: "The *vrykolakas* begins with his own beard."

Particularly in the case of loved ones, broken vows could doom corpses to wander above the now-alien ground, seeking forgiveness or vindication. Such was the case once on a Greek island in the Sporades, where small stone houses climbed pine-covered hills above harbors.

In one of these towns lived an elderly woman, bent and black-robed in the widow's weeds to be seen everywhere in that hard land. This woman, however, was rich in children: She had nine strong sons, who farmed the olive groves outside the town for her, and one daughter, whose name was Areté.

She doted upon her pretty daughter, and when a sea trader offered for the maiden, the mother hesitated, although the man was kind and generous, and promised a fine bride price as well. Areté would be taken far away: The trader came from Persia. She consulted with her sons. The youngest, Constantine by

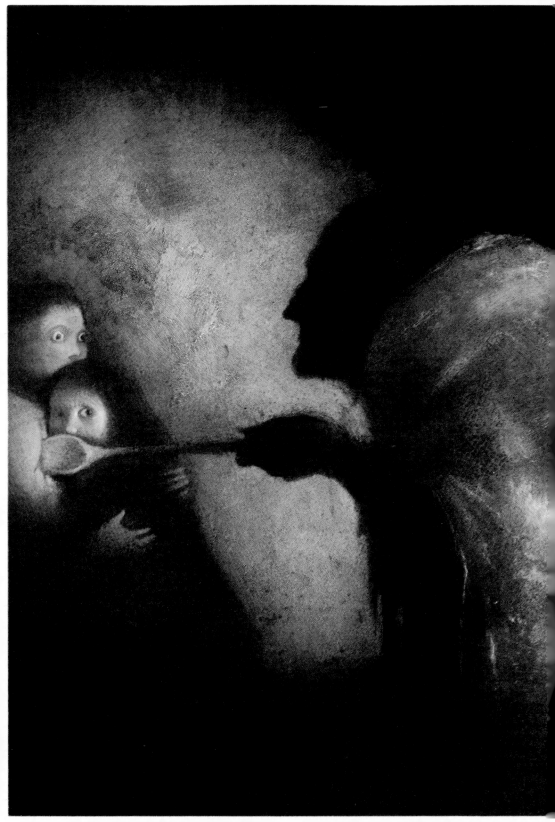

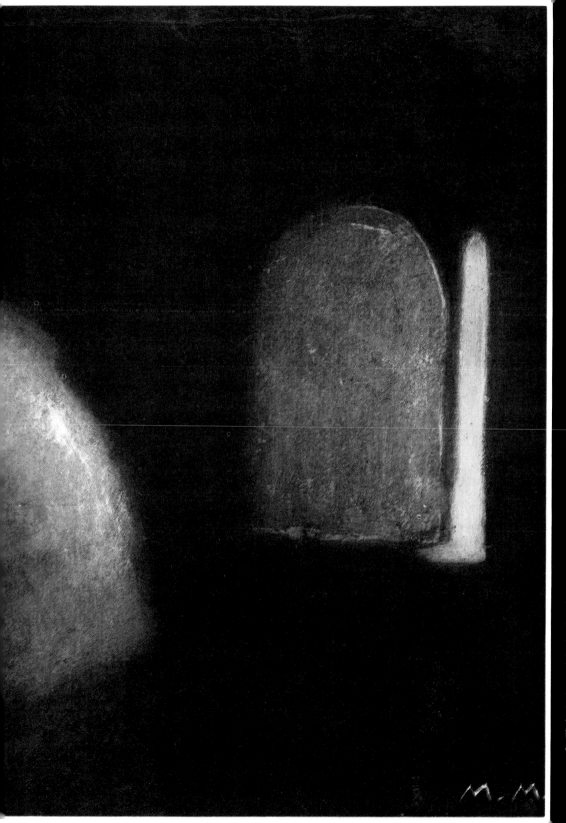

## Child-eater of the Black Forest

Most of the tales for children pain
the world in cheerful hues, but a few
see to the very center of evil. One tells
of a brother and sister trapped by a
flesh-eating ghoul.

The children, Hansel and Gretel
by name, were abandoned by their
parents in a German wood during a
time of famine, when the adults them
selves were starving and had no food
for younger mouths. Left alone, the
two simply wandered among the trees.
They might have gone on until they
dropped, had they not come upon a
small house, carved in the ornate fash
ion of the region and flanked by a
squat chimney that gave forth a fra
grant ribbon of smoke. Smoke meant
cooking. The children scratched at the
door, unashamed to beg.

A pair of long arms instantly
pulled them inside. The thing that
gripped them bore the raddled face o
a crone. She locked the door; they
were her prisoners now.

At least they were fed. Day after
day, the crone gave them gruel. Day
after day, muttering and chuckling to
herself, she poked at them with bony
fingers, cruelly pinching the flesh as if
to test it. A day came at last when she
busied herself with the bellows at her
deep oven. She spoke to the children
from time to time, repeating the same
gloating refrain: "I like my meat
cooked." When all was ready she
dragged them to the oven mouth. But
the children were stronger now, hav
ing been fed for many days to fatten
them up. According to the story, they
succeeded in pushing the crone into
her own oven and slamming it shut.

It was said that Hansel and Gretel
then found the old woman's gold and
took it to their parents, so they never
were hungry again, but this may have
been an invention, made for the sake
of lightening the tale's savage truths.

## A vampire's disguises

Possessed of every weapon of stealth and evil, vampires were formidably skilled at changing shape. They did not, as is sometimes believed, change into bats: This metamorphosis was a literary invention, added to vampire tales after the discovery of New World bats that fed on blood. But to move undetected from place to place, vampires could dissolve to dust or mist, sail through the air as owls and run along the ground as wolves or cats.

The vampires of Japan particularly favored the last transformation. These night roamers, said to frequent the courts of early Japanese princes, presented the relatively innocent appearance of court concubines at most times and, in this guise, drained the lifeblood of their lovers. If startled or pursued, however, they dwindled in size, dropped their kimonos and emerged from the silken folds as large, swift cats, marked as vampires by the fact that they had two tails.

name, persuaded her to let the maiden go. He smiled in his careless, bright way and swore that if ever the mother wished for Areté, whether in bitterness or joy, he himself would fetch her home.

So Areté left her island, and the mother and sons went on as before, although the mother never ceased to mourn her girl. She took to brooding and to staring out over the sea, as if longing and watching would return her daughter to her or bring word from Areté in her distant home. But the sea returned only silence; all the comfort she had in her mourning was the company of her sons and the promise of Constantine.

And the time came she had not even that. Pestilence beset the island, brought on some trader's ship. The nature of the disease is not recorded, only that it spread swiftly and killed horribly. One by one the woman's sons fell ill, and one by one

they died. She was left alone in her small house, aged and empty-hearted. More than ever, she longed for Areté, and inwardly she raged at Constantine, who could not now keep his vow.

To ease her grief, she climbed one night to the pine groves where her dead were buried. She stood for hours by the mounded graves, and presently she began to whisper and then to wail. Finally, she went to the foot of Constantine's grave, and she called down on him the ancient curses of the Greeks.

"Constantine the faithless son," she cried. "Hear thy mother's words! May thou not rest; may thou remain incorrupt. May the ground receive thee not. May the black earth spew thee out."

Then she fell silent. She waited, but no answer came, and at last she turned and hobbled down the hill. At her back the earth above the grave shifted and trembled; pine needles scattered as the ground cracked. A hand fumbled at the crack, and then a head appeared, blackened and distorted. The corpse of Constantine had risen from the dead. It cleared the ground and stumbled through the trees, clinging to shadow. Down the hill it loped, making for the harbor below.

But the mother did not see this. Spent with her cursings, she made her slow way home, closed the door and lay on her wall bench to die. For three nights she lay sleepless and rigid, staring at the ceiling. She ate nothing and drank nothing.

On the fourth night, her door blew loudly open. Standing on the threshold was her daughter, Areté, wind-racked and white-faced and apparently oblivious of the blackened thing that stood beside her.

The mother saw it, however, and knew it for what it was. Her heart swelled with joy at the sight of her daughter, but she had a duty to the silent creature that had been her son — a faithful son, after all — and she did the duty in the time-honored fashion of her people. She rose, threw a handful of salt into a water jar that stood in the room and flung the water on the *vrykolakas*, crying aloud as she did so, "As this salt dissolves, so does my curse. Rest, and walk no more."

The blackened thing shuddered. The swollen flesh split and shredded so that the bones showed through; then the bones themselves crumbled. With no more than a faint crackling and pattering, the body of Constantine dissolved to a handful of dust.

As for the mother, having released her son to his final rest, she died in her daughter's arms.

How the *vrykolakas* had achieved its goal and fulfilled its promise no one could tell; it seemed that the creature had flown. But fulfill its promise it had. Like many other vampires of that early time, it rose because it was forced to rise, not because of malign intent.

As ages passed, however, the Aegean world was contaminated by evil from the north. From the plains and mountain fastnesses of Bulgaria, Rumania and Hungary came lost souls, hungrily searching out the dead, whose flesh would house them and give them strength. They filtered into Greece, and when they did, the *vrykolakes*

began to change in character. They became killers, aimlessly searching for lives to take, in the manner of vampires from the northern lands.

The killing instinct was strong there, and the vampires so numerous as to constitute an army of the night. In Bulgaria, for instance, the death thirst ran in families, and the patterns of transformations after death were known to everyone. A member of such a family rose from the grave nine days after burial, not as flesh but as shadow — a phantom shape that blocked the light and showed itself in showers of sparks at night. It was called an *obour*. Too weak as yet to kill, such creatures roamed villages, tormenting the inhabitants with shriekings in the streets. They smeared walls with cow dung and spat blood on floors.

These manifestations were frightening and disgusting, but they did not threaten life. After forty days, however, the *obours* slipped back into their bodies, then rose from the tomb and went among the living again, this time with lethal effect. By night they hunted, leaving behind a trail of dying animals and dying people.

They killed because they had to: Only with long draughts of fresh blood could vampires continue to survive. This overwhelming need gave them a perpetual hunger, and it was the reason for the hideous appearance that vampires presented. They had clawlike fingernails that caught and held victims; sharp teeth that plunged smoothly into arteries and veins; and full, eager lips that closed and sucked in measured rhythm. Each night when they fed, their ashen flesh acquired the rosy glow of

If a Bulgarian villager saw a shadow that was vaguely human in shape but
        not cast by any mortal, he knew he stood at risk, for the shadow was the fledgling
   form of a vampire. When the creature grew strong, it would become a killer.

health, flushing with the color that seeped from their mortal victims.

In their dependence on blood, vampires reflected, in a perverted way, the most profound of mortal beliefs. Humankind from earliest times revered blood's magic vivifying power and cherished it as the most precious of substances, the river of the life force. The highest sacrifice that could be made was that of the blood of living creatures. Thus, the altars of gods were spattered with scarlet, and the fields of the farmers were drenched before plowing. Among the Norse, even sailing vessels were consecrated with blood: The Vikings ran their longships over the bodies of prisoners before sailing, so that the keels might be reddened to honor their seagods. (The drenching of a keel with wine at a ship's christening is a kinder, cleaner memory of this brutal custom.)

Enhancing its worth was the belief that the blood of any being carried the qualities of that being and could transmit those qualities if drunk. Viking warriors drank the blood of bears to gain the beasts' ferocious strength. And the dead, in drinking the lifeblood of the living, acquired something of life itself.

It was said that the Greek hero Odysseus once visited the world of the dead to find the Theban seer Tiresias and learn the course of the future from him. Odysseus discovered only shades—pale, flitting, formless beings without even the power of speech. Only when the living man killed a sheep and fed its blood to the ghost of the prophet did Tiresias acquire the substance and voice to tell the living hero that his voyages would be filled with danger, as indeed they were.

As the centuries wore on, vampires wandered every point of the earth in their endless search for sustenance. Ireland, for example, was haunted by the Dearg-due, or "Red Bloodsucker"—a pale young woman who lingered in graveyards at night, waiting for unwary passersby. Her beauty was irresistibly seductive, but when she kissed, she fed on blood, draining the life from her victims.

In Scotland, such creatures were called *baobhan sith*, and they lurked with others of their kind in the mountain wilds. The Scots were fond of telling tales of encounters with these creatures, and the tales were not pleasant ones.

A man named McPhee once related how he had hunted on a winter's day with three companions in the western Highlands. Evening found the party many miles from home, and the men decided to take shelter in an abandoned shieling, the rustic lean-to used in those parts to shelter sheep during the summer grazing season. The men built a small fire to roast the rabbits they had caught, and the dark little hut soon grew pleasantly warm. The whisky jar passed from hand to hand. Presently, McPhee began the lilting, wordless humming called *puirt-a-beul*, which Highlanders enjoyed. His companions rose and danced in the darkness to his melody.

Round and round they danced, clumsy with laughter and flushed with drink. After a while, McPhee paused for breath, and his companions, red-faced with exertion

One dark night, recalls a Scottish tale, a group of huntsmen fell prey to baobhan sith—women vampires who roamed the Highlands. The vampires whirled the men in a dance of death and drank their blood as they trod the lively measures.

paused too. "You trip a bonny measure," observed McPhee.

"Aye," replied one of his companions with a leer and a wink. "And it would be bonnier still if we had pretty maids to trip it with us."

Outside the shieling, the wind rose; a hound howled once; the hunters' horses stamped and whinnied. Then the door blew open. The men turned quickly at the sound, and were astonished at the sight it heralded.

Four lovely maidens, all clothed in green, stood in the entrance. One of them fixed McPhee with a bright, red-rimmed eye. With little clicking steps she minced to his side. She put her hand on his shoulder and nodded, and willy-nilly he resumed his singing.

His companions, blank-faced as if enchanted, began to dance to his measure, but they were slow and awkward now, for each was held fast in clinging arms: The maidens danced with them. Not a word was spoken. The only sounds were the clicking of the women's feet, the leafy rustle of their dresses and the reedy hum of McPhee's dancing song.

How long he sang and his fellows danced, McPhee could not tell. At some point, however, the song dried in his throat. The women's mouths were fastened on the necks of his friends; blood bubbled at the pretty lips and spotted the men's shirts.

With a howl, McPhee bolted. Out the door he ran, into the night, and the woman who had stood beside him followed.

He could not shake her; he later swore he had seen her feet and that they were the hoofs of a deer. He felt her breath on his neck, and her fingernails dug into his arm. He wrenched free and dashed among the tethered horses.

For reasons he did not understand, she seemed unable to approach him once he was among the animals. There he stood, leaning on their warm flanks, for the remainder of the night. In the darkness, he heard her footsteps and hissing breath, but all such evidence of her lurking presence faded with the morning light.

Not until the sun was well up did McPhee stir, however. He left the horses cautiously, looking around him all the while, and peered into the shieling. The fire was out, the little space quite dark. McPhee stepped in and saw his hunting mates. They lay on the ground—pale, bloodless corpses. The ragged, bitten flesh on their throats was crusted and dry.

Such hauntings and killings were not uncommon once, and everywhere the pattern was roughly the same: Vampires seemed to seduce their victims, most of whom submitted helplessly to the predatory embrace, as if enspelled. Some vampires drained their prey at once; some took a little blood each night so that the men and women they feasted on wasted slowly, day by day. In Slavic lands there were cases of villages that appeared to be infested by vampires. Whole populations faded in these places, and died bloodless.

Faced with silent enemies—enemies invisible by day, for in the sunlit hours, vampires retired to their graves or assumed the shapes of neighbors or animals—men and women walked in fear. They carried amulets for protection. Objects of iron, for example, were anathema to all evil spirits, as were crucifixes. No one knew why, but garlic—long believed potent against poison and infection—also repelled vampires, and it could be carried or worn in bags suspended from the neck.

But these measures were not enough. For real safety, vampires had to be caught by day, when they were helpless, and physically destroyed. They had first, of course, to be found—a challenge that gave rise to certain bizarre trades. In the vampire-haunted Balkan Mountains dwelled scores of vampire hunters, most of them charlatans. Some claimed to be sorcerers and said they could trap vampire spirits in bottles; they would carry out an elaborate pretense of such a capture, then charge a handsome fee. Other such specialists, peculiar to Serbia, were called *dhampirs*; these were supposed to be sons sired by vampires and therefore gifted with peculiar powers over them. *Dhampirs* were paid to seek vampires by day and battle them to the death in public—an easily staged fraud, since the vampires of Serbia were visible only to the eyes of their offspring.

In fact, the ways of finding vampires were few and simple. If they walked in the bodies of dead loved ones, they might be recognized; or they might be exposed by the fact that they cast neither shadow nor reflection. Once the creature was detected, it might be traced to a grave where it rested during the day. Sometimes vampires were seen entering their earthen beds; sometimes their names were known and, in those cases, tracing the grave was not difficult. In other cases, crypts and graveyards had to be searched for signs of unnatural life.

In some countries this was done with the aid of a ritual: A young boy was mounted on a pure white stallion that had never been put to stud, and the virginal pair was led over each grave in a churchyard. The animal would balk at a grave that contained a vampire. Then the hunters would dig. When the coffin was reached and its lid removed, one glance at the corpse within was enough to confirm the matter. The living dead showed none of the usual signs of decay; instead, they lay firm and rosy, swollen like leeches with blood from their unholy feedings.

At this point, any of several methods might be used to put an end to the vampire's wanderings. The mildest was to turn the body face down and rebury it, so that the creature would claw in the wrong direction if it attempted to leave the grave again. In some countries, vampires were pinned to the earth with a stake through the heart. Or the head might be cut off and placed between the legs. The most certain way of destroying a vampire forever was to burn the corpse to ashes, but even this was not without its dangers, as a Russian story tells.

The tale concerns a Cossack from the Ukraine who, when the adventure began, was returning from his home to join his regiment. He walked for many days along a track that led through the vast Ukrainian wheat fields, now all harvested and

## Impaling the borrowed body

Brutal means were used to put an end to the ravages of vampires. The graves of suspect corpses were opened to see if decay had done its natural work. If instead, the bodies were fresh and full of blood, people knew they housed a vampire spirit. Evidence from old burials reveals the sort of action fearful folk took then. To rob the corpses of the power to walk, the leg tendons might be cut. Sometimes the heads were severed and placed between the thighs. Or vampires might be pinned to the ground by driving stakes of hawthorne or ash through the hearts or skulls. A nail of iron—always proof against evil—was better. It was said that the torrents of blood from such corpses rose like fountains in the air.

reduced to brown stubble. The way was lonely and cold and the skies mostly gray. Occasionally the wavering arrow-heads of flocks of geese passed over, heading for a warmer land.

Sometimes the soldier saw farmers in the fields; sometimes he came upon a village where he could find a barn to sleep in and food to eat before he moved on, but this was rare. The villages were widely scattered, and in their isolation, the people of the region had become fearful and unwelcoming. They regarded the Cossack with suspicion and crossed themselves three times at his approach.

He was cheered, therefore, on an evening of gathering twilight, to see the glow of a small fire beside the road ahead: Another traveler might be welcome company.

He marched briskly to the place. A man clothed in fluttering rags sat by the warming flames, mending a pair of shabby boots. This stranger was no coward. He had built his campfire beside a graveyard.

"Ho, brother," said the Cossack, and went to the fire to warm his hands.

The stranger watched him from shadowed eyes and replied that he called no man kin. Then he bent to his mending again, saying nothing further. Undaunted by the churlishness, the Cossack continued to warm his hands.

At length, the stranger rose and put on his boots. Without a word, he threw dirt on the fire to quench it. When the flames died, he turned his back on the Cossack and set off down the road.

"I will walk with you," the soldier said, and fell easily into step beside the stranger. "Where do you go?"

The stranger shrugged and responded, "I go to find amusement."

It soon became clear that there was amusement to be had. The lights of a village twinkled ahead of them, and the sound of singing floated on the night air.

Quickening their steps, the two men presently arrived at a cottage whose door stood welcomingly open to the night. The travelers had arrived in the midst of a village wedding. The scene was very gay inside the little house. A fire blazed, and the long table was laden. The bride in her embroidered tunic and beribboned headdress blushed and smiled and greeted the strangers kindly, while gathered all around her the wedding guests sang the lengthy choruses of some of the best-loved songs of the region.

Well provided for, the Cossack prepared to enjoy himself. He sat at the table and sang with the others and for some hours he failed to notice the activities of

. . . The villagers burned the trapped vampire to ashes. But even as
the host-body withered, the demon spirit sought freedom, leaping
from the flames in the form of serpents and other swift creatures. . . .

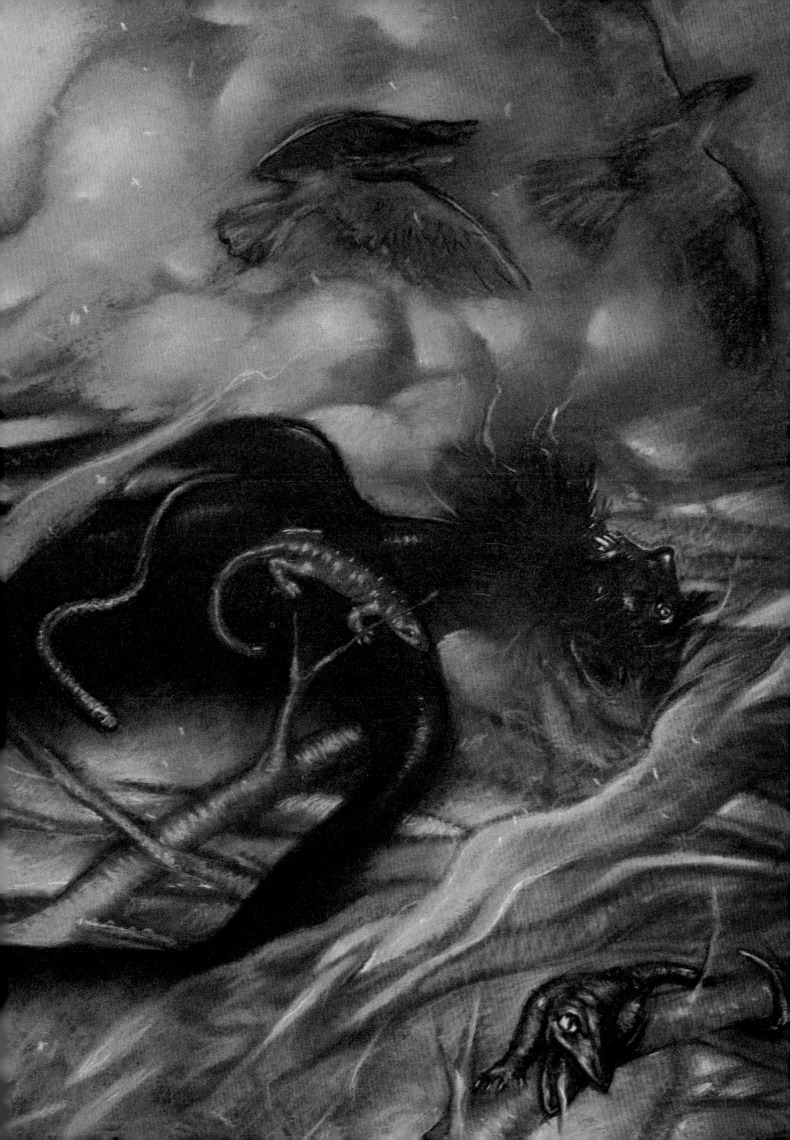

his companion, who seemed to prefer the periphery, clinging to shadows in corners, as though he were ashamed of his rags.

In the hours after midnight, the stranger approached the bride where she sat surrounded by the company. He knelt before her as if in homage or in supplication, and when she put out her hands to raise him, he buried his face in them. The Cossack saw the tableau clearly in the firelight: The rosy maiden, the pale and ragged wanderer kneeling before her, the faces of the laughing company behind.

Then the picture was broken. The stranger, his own face flushed now, rose. He turned on his heel and left the cottage swiftly, and as he vanished through the door, the young woman swooned. At once she was surrounded by her family, but the Cossack did not stay to help them lift her. He had seen the stranger's face quite clearly, and he followed the man into the night.

The Cossack found the ragged man not many yards down the road, walking quickly, but not so quickly that a soldier could not catch up with him. In a moment, the Cossack had seized the stranger's arm to halt him.

"I know you for what you are," the Cossack said softly.

The stranger jerked his arm away. A fearful stench rose from his clothing. His lips stretched tight in a death's-head grin that showed the blood clotting at the corners of his mouth.

"Leave me, mortal," he said coldly. "I have fed, and I am strong. I might wish to feed again."

But the soldier merely laughed, and punched the stranger in the chest. The man coughed and spat. Then he began to run, with the Cossack on his heels.

At the graveyard, by the ashes of his fire, the stranger turned at bay.

"What we do with vampires is we burn them," said the Cossack in a conversational tone. Then he hit the stranger again.

Surprisingly, the creature laughed. "The thing that lives in me can escape the fire and reside in other bodies, fool," he shouted, and he wound long arms around the soldier's waist.

The Cossack smashed his fists into the creature's face and felt bone break. Blood bubbled from the creature's mouth, and the stranger's jaw hung askew, but he held the Cossack fast. They fell to the ground, panting, and rolled among the graves, kicking, punching, clawing and biting.

The Cossack later said he could not reckon how much time passed while they fought. The battle went on in an ever-slower rhythm as he tired, fighting mechanically, without thought.

Acock's crow saved him. It came from the village, where the fowl were stirring at first light. When the raucous cry sounded, the vampire froze where he lay. Then he gave the soldier a mighty shove and rolled free, sliding like a shadow into a nearby grave.

The soldier walked slowly back to the hamlet, nursing his wounds. He roused the villagers and told what he had seen. Soon the menfolk were gathered around the grave, armed with scythes and shovels and accompanied by a cart bearing a heavy load of ash and birch.

*. . . If from the pyre of a vampire even one creature escaped, the vampire spirit would survive. All too soon, it would find another host and rise to walk again among the living.*

They dug down through the earth and lifted out the coffin. It was not fastened. They pushed the lid aside and there, within the coffin, lay the stranger, his jaw broken, his head twisted at an insane angle. His eyes were open. They gleamed malevolently at the faces that looked down on him, but the vampire did not move, and no sound came from the crimson, swollen lips.

The villagers built a funeral pyre in the graveyard and, using pitchforks rather than their hands, heaved the hateful body onto it. They watched for hours—chanting prayers, shouting curses and adding logs whenever the fire weakened—while the vampire's skin blackened and blistered and the ragged clothes withered to ash. At last even the denuded skeleton began to crumble, and as it did a high and guttural howl rose from the flames and seemed to hover in the air.

At once there came other sounds, a scampering and rustling as a host of vermin poured from the fire—serpents and lizards, glistening maggots, swollen rats, and broad-winged scavenger birds. With their shovels and scythes the villagers beat at the creatures, severing heads, crushing spines. As quickly as they could, they shoveled the twitching little bodies back into the flames to burn, and as quickly as they did, more beasts scuttled out onto the earth, dodging frantically between the stamping feet and swinging implements of the mortals, heading swiftly for the long stubble of the autumn fields and the dark and distant woods, where hiding places and safety lay.

The killing went on for many hours, but at last the creatures stopped coming, and the villagers let the fire go out. After the vampire's ashes were scattered in the cold wind, they headed for home and the safety of their hearths.

They had vanquished the night creature, or so they thought. The Cossack went on with his journey after some days, and never passed that way again. He never discovered whether every one of the crawling, slithering, flying creatures had been returned to the fire. Had a single one escaped, the vampire's spirit would have escaped with it and roamed secretly in the wild until it found a new host to give it human form.

The odds were much in favor of the vampire. Blood devourers were a protean breed, and any victory over them was no more than temporary. Like other night creatures, they were informed by a terrible spirit: Their bodies could be destroyed, but that spirit could survive somewhere, nurtured by the darkness, to be reborn one night in another time and place, under a different skin.

# Nightstalker of Croglin Grange

For centuries, a low stone house called Croglin Grange crouched peaceably on its hillock in the northwest of England, commanding a fine view of rolling moor and of a churchyard that lay in a declivity below the grounds. Many generations of a family named Fisher lived undisturbed at the grange; in fact, it was only in the early 19th Century, when the youngest Fishers left the place for a larger house, that Croglin Grange earned its reputation as a place of horror.

During the months that followed the Fishers' departure, the house stood silent and untenanted. When winter passed and spring came, however, laughter echoed in the little drawing room, and the old-fashioned leaded windows stood open to the sunlight once more. The grange had been let to a family named Cranswell.

The Cranswells—two brothers and their sister—were a merry crew indeed; they were pleased with the venerable house and delighted with the country air. They had nothing but good to report to the villagers who lived nearby, to the farmers who supplied them with milk and eggs, and to the young people from neighboring houses with whom they dined and rode and picnicked. If any of the Cranswells noticed the various signs of violence that gamekeepers had begun to talk about—small hares torn and bloodied, birds plucked bare and drained of blood—not one of them mentioned the fact.

But the Cranswell family soon would suffer at the hands of the thing that roamed the grounds of Croglin Grange.

Their adventure began at dusk one summer evening. Miss Cranswell retired to her chamber and lingered by the window, watching the last light fade across the sloping lawn outside and pool in shadows in the hollow where the churchyard lay. Two small, flamelike lights danced among the darkening gravestones—will-o'-the-wisps, perhaps. She stared at them, and as she stared, they moved across the churchyard wall; free of that confinement, they floated in aimless fashion at the bottom of the lawn. Unnerved, Miss Cranswell pulled the window closed and latched it. Then she bolted the door and got into bed.

She sat propped against the pillows for some moments, listening, but all she heard were the creakings of the old house as it settled for the night. At last she smiled at her own timidity and closed her eyes.

Suddenly she was jolted awake again. Something rustled at the window and rattled at the latch. Outside the casement, two points of light shone, refracted by the glass panes. It was clear, at these close quarters, that the lights were the eyes of a man-shaped creature. While she gazed, transfixed, a shadowy hand rapped softly on a windowpane.

Miss Cranswell opened her mouth to scream, but no sound came. Frozen by fear, she watched the hand explore the window frame and panes. Presently the sound of scratching echoed in the room. The creature was picking away the lead that sealed a pane.

With a crash, the pane fell out. The hand, necrotically gray, reached through

the space and lifted the window latch. Then the window swung open, and Miss Cranswell's visitor stood fully revealed.

He was a pale man, so pale that his face gave the effect of a network of cobwebs, except for the glowing eyes and fleshy, crimson lips. His head swung from side to side as he surveyed the room; then, nimble and silent as a spider, he leaped over the window sill and across the floor to the side of Miss Cranswell's bed.

He loomed over the bed, swaying slightly. Motionless where she lay, Miss Cranswell looked up at him with blank eyes. Then, as gently as a lover, he twined his withered hands in her hair, forcing her head back. His lips drew apart, the incisors gleaming white. Then he bent down, as if to bestow a kiss.

The conclusion of this scene was later described by Miss Cranswell's brothers. Evidently she found her voice at last, for a high-pitched, wavering scream echoed through the quiet halls of Croglin Grange. Within seconds, the young men were at their sister's door. It was locked. They set their shoulders to it and knocked it down.

The brothers found an appalling sight. Ashen-faced, their sister lay against her pillows. Narrow streams of scarlet arterial blood pumped feebly from her throat, mingling with darker, bluish trickles from severed veins and staining the white linen by her head. Only the faint twitching of her arms and legs beneath the bedclothes showed that she still lived.

Bent on saving Miss Cranswell's life if they could, the brothers merely noted the

open window and broken windowpane. Later, they remembered the odor of mold and the sweet stench that overlay it in the room. At the time, however, their energies were devoted to stanching the flow of blood and summoning aid.

They were successful. Miss Cranswell survived the attack, and as soon as she was strong enough, her brothers closed the house and took her to Switzerland to recuperate in the mountain air.

Not many months passed, however, before the family returned to Croglin Grange. Having heard their sister's tale, the young men suspected what kind of creature had wounded her, and they were set on destroying it. To their dismay, Miss Cranswell, who seems to have been an intrepid woman, insisted on helping them.

On a winter's night, therefore, she lay once more in her bedchamber and waited for the moon to rise. Once more, twin flames gleamed in the darkness outside. Once more, Miss Cranswell heard scratching at the windowpane and saw the glass fall and the casement swing open.

But this time she was not alone. Her brothers, armed with pocket pistols, waited with her, and as the vampire rose to the window sill, they fired. At once, the creature dropped from sight. All the Cranswells heard then was a whining howl; all they saw was a dark figure scuttling across the lawn, making for the churchyard.

Together, the Cranswells waited out the watches of the night, for they did not care to venture abroad when one of the demons of the night was loose. At first

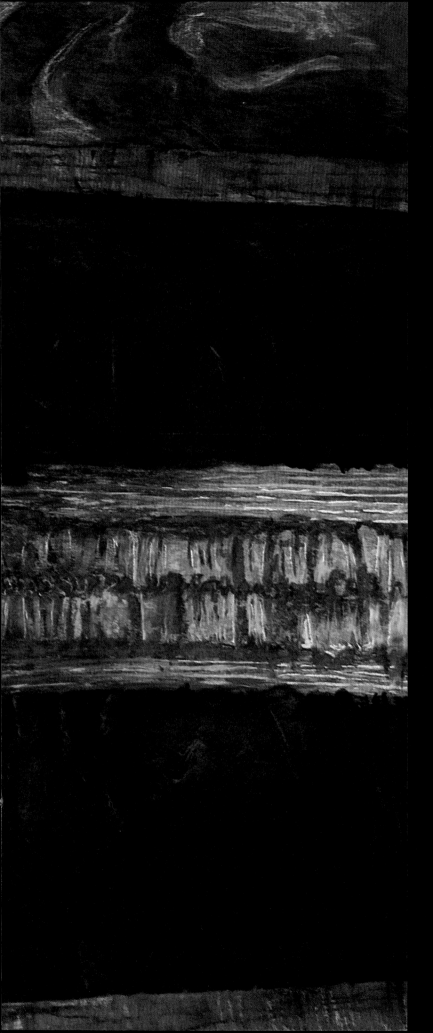

light, the brothers took Miss Cranswell to a neighboring farm. Then, with the farmer and his men, they walked to the churchyard below Croglin Grange.

The place was quiet, the tombs undisturbed. The men searched the church; nothing was to be seen in the nave. Near the altar, however, was a stone door that led to the crypt beneath the church, and behind that door, a dreadful scene waited.

The coffins in the crypt had been desecrated—torn from their niches and broken open. Their piteous contents—bones for the most part, fragmented and scarred with the marks of human teeth—lay scattered on the stone floor.

One coffin alone was undisturbed, although it stood open. In the coffin, as still as the dead, lay the visitor to Croglin Grange, pale of face and red of lip. His eyes were open, but no fire lighted them; like all vampires, he was powerless during the daylight hours. One leg was freshly bloodied by a bullet wound.

In grim silence, the men did what they must. They dragged the coffin from the crypt into the now-sunny churchyard, and there they burned it to ashes, so that the vampire could not strike again.

No one ever discovered where the creature came from or why it preyed upon the Cranswell family when it had left the Fishers alone. When the villagers were asked about it, they shrugged and turned away: Such inexplicable hauntings were not uncommon once. But the Cranswells left Croglin Grange, and the house remained empty for many years afterward.

# Chapter Four

# The Way of the Werebeast

In a century long past, the aged fortress town of Magdeburg in Prussian Saxony presented a deceptively comfortable appearance. Sited on the Elbe River, Magdeburg was a place of steep-roofed, half-timbered houses and barge-crowded canals. Streets paved with cobblestones laced the town's center and fanned out higgledy-piggledy to the surrounding grainfields. Beyond the fields, however, loomed another country: the wolf-haunted slopes of the Harz Mountains. The little town was a sunny island in a sea of shadows, but it was not proof against the old magic that lurked in the high pine forests, as events of a certain winter showed.

The incidents began in January, when the canals lay locked in ice, the snow-muffled streets glowed blue in the early twilight, and good folk stayed close to their warm stoves, shutting their ears against the winds that moaned down from the mountains. A child disappeared one night from its nursery, and then the following night, another child from another house, and the next night yet another. No cry was

M. M.

heard; nothing in the little rooms was disturbed. But clues to the children's fate were found soon enough. Outside the houses in the snow were tracks with four clawed toes and distinctive, triangular pads—the unmistakable prints of a wolf. Then the townsfolk spoke of winters past when the beasts had left their forests and slunk into the streets of the town in search of food. January was called in those parts *Wolf-monat*, or "wolf month," because starving wolves walked among men then.

But wolves hunted in pairs or packs, and the tracks in Magdeburg were those of one animal only. And what wolf struck silently? What wolf crossed human thresholds to spirit children away?

All of these questions were repeatedly put to the magistrate of Magdeburg, whose name was Breber, as he dealt with his frantic neighbors in the weeks that followed. He had no answers. He ordered curfews; he posted armed men in the streets, but still the night thief triumphed. The children of the town continued to vanish—servants' children, tradesmen's children, bargemen's children, lockkeepers' children. And it was not only the humbler households that suffered: The barrister's infant son was taken; so was the daughter of the fortress's commander.

The people of Magdeburg passed from appeal to reproach. Having no scapegoat, they turned on their magistrate as if the blame were somehow his. Even his golden-haired wife, who had no children to lose, seemed to reject him. At the beginning of the troubles, she had begun to withdraw from him. Now she kept to her own rooms and denied him her bed at night. He saw very little of her.

This grieved him, but Breber was a conscientious man and a brave one. He left his wife to her solitude and, armed with a sword, patrolled the cold streets at night himself. For the most part, he saw no one except the guards he had posted, who greeted him sullenly or not at all as he marched his lonely rounds.

A night came, however, when someone accosted him on the street. It was an evening dense with snow fog, and Breber had some difficulty finding his direction in the narrow lanes and twisting alleyways of the poor section where he walked. At length, he paused to get his bearings and light his pipe, and when he did so, a small form hurled itself upon him.

He seized it, and it took shape in the darkness. It was a disheveled woman, wrapped in rags. He recognized her. She had been among the first to lose a child, and the loss had unsettled her mind. She wandered the streets now, raving.

Breber steadied the woman and bent his head to listen.

"The night has teeth," she gabbled in a hoarse whisper. "The night has claws, and I have found them."

Breber dropped his hands. At once, the woman turned and lurched off down the street through the thick mist, whining and mumbling. With a sigh, the magistrate followed her. In fact, her course seemed to have direction, although it was a convoluted one. It led through the mean little suburb, out to the town's fringes and across the snow-blanketed grainfields.

With Breber trailing behind, she went into the pines, taking a path that he himself had taken while hunting during the previous autumn. She ranged from side to side along the path like a dog on a scent. Then she turned sharply to one side and plunged into ice-glazed underbrush.

After a moment, she gave a crow of triumph, and Breber in that instant saw her prey—a darkly shrouded figure, loping on all fours, bearing in its mouth a bulky burden. She set off after it, so swiftly that Breber lost sight of her. Her scuffling track was easy to follow, however: Outside the town, the air was very clear, and moonlight glittered on the snow. Drawing his sword, Breber gave chase.

The trail ended some moments later in a clearing that Breber knew well: It held a hunting lodge that he sometimes used. He heard the woman's trembling screams long before he reached the place, and under those screams rumbled bestial growls.

Without hesitation, Breber plunged toward the door and crashed through it.

The rustic lodge had become a slaughterhouse. Amid a litter of small bones lay the mangled body of the woman he had followed. Half her face was gone, and a single eye stared sightlessly at the ceiling. Her clothes had been ripped away, and her entrails snaked and pulsed across her belly. She twitched, gurgled, and was still.

Hunched over the body, close by the shivering form of a small child, was her killer. Breber reeled backward at the sight: It was a thing something more than an animal but something less than a human, and even as Breber stared, its shape appeared to shift horribly between the two. It had the head of a wolf and a wolf's cold and glittering eyes, but from its bared fangs blood dripped down onto the swelling white bosom of a woman. From the massive head, golden curls dropped grotesquely onto hairy gray shoulders. From a woman's pale hands, enormous lupine claws curled.

The thing raised its head and, with a snarl, lunged. But Breber was quicker. He thrust his sword into the beast-woman's heart and held the hilt with hands of iron while the creature screamed and writhed upon the blade. It fell at last at his feet, and the magistrate wrenched the sword back and raised it to sever the head.

But the blade never descended. Beneath his uncomprehending stare, a terrible change came over the beast. Its fur faded and melted in the air; its form trembled and straightened; and a woman, not a wolf or half-wolf, lay before Breber on the bloodied floor.

She raised a feeble hand to him. Then the hand fell back, and the light in her eyes faded. The woman was Breber's wife.

After a while, Breber picked up the now-wailing child and left the place. Weeping, he carried the child back to Magdeburg and told the townsfolk what had happened. He left them to dispose of his wife's body, and he never spoke of her again.

But the townspeople spoke of her for many years. They said that in the autumn, when Breber's wife had hunted with her husband in the Harz Mountains, she had drunk water from a mountain spring and paid a fearful price.

*For the creatures called werewolves, the thrill of attaining animal power came at
the price of agony. In the transformation, stiff hair pierced human flesh, sharp
fangs burst through human gums, and lust for killing fouled the human heart.*

Some of the waters that bubbled to the surface there were said to flow from an ancient source deep in the earth. The water was impregnated with the dark magic of another age, a time older than towns, older even than the forests themselves. A single cooling draught could leave its poison within forever. The hapless humans who drank from certain brooks or springs forfeited half of their humanity. They spent their days in human shape and their nights in the form of murderous beasts, reminders to the orderly new world of the powers of a wilder era.

All unwittingly, Breber's wife had joined a secret and fearsome company of the night. She had become a werewolf, a name derived from the Anglo-Saxon *were*, or "man"; such creatures were literally human wolves. There were many of her kind. Although men and women had long grown beyond their fellow animals, had built such thriving towns as Magdeburg and sent great cathedrals soaring skyward to celebrate the soul—that invisible essence that set them above the beasts— traces of the beast remained in them and could be called forth.

In every part of the earth appeared creatures who lived alternately as men or women and as animals, borrowing the shapes of predators that plagued their particular homelands. Thus, from parts of Europe where wild boars, bears and wolves roamed came tales of men who assumed the shapes of boars, bears or wolves and preyed on kin and neighbors. In India, people feared the weretiger. Shadowy werefoxes roamed China and Japan.

Some of these creatures were cursed from birth to lose their humanity at intervals. Some, like Breber's wife, were victims of enchantment. And some deliberately chose the way of animal powers and the freedom of the wild. It was said, for example, that certain sorcerers and witches learned from Satan how to transform themselves into animal guise. They rubbed themselves with unguents composed of such ingredients as baby's fat and poisonous hemlock, henbane and deadly nightshade. Among Teutonic peoples, it was thought that donning special girdles made of the pelt of a wolf or the skin of a hanged man would effect the change. In the Balkans, the magic came from drinking water from a beast's footprint, or from eating a beast's brain.

The people who practiced these magics surrendered their humanity for the sake of power. Their world was a hard one. Most led lives tightly bound by obedience to divine or mundane authority and often beset by famine, war or disease. But those who became werebeasts left the puny prison of the human form; they ran free in a dark world sharp with scents and busy with secret sounds. Throwing off the fetters of reason and sensibility, casting aside the dilemmas of human choice, blessed with the swiftness and strength and cunning of a beast, the humblest of them became lords of the forest—and of their former fellows, when they chose.

From earliest times, in fact, men had sought the power of beasts. It was in the hope of acquiring such strength, for instance, that the fighting men of many

tribes wore animal skins into battle. Among Norse armies were warriors who sought to capture animal power by cloaking themselves in the hide of a bear. From the word for this garment – *bearsark*, or "bear shirt" – they took their name: berserkers. Enemies facing such a foe on the field of battle found nothing human in the sight. The bear-men, naked beneath their thick pelts, howled and pranced. They ground their teeth and flung themselves into battle with reckless, mindless fury. And the moment would come when the fury mastered them and an ancient power flowed. In the fullness of his animal ecstasy, it was said, a berserker could bite through the iron of a shield or plunge through fire without pain.

The wolf was and is another animal of great power. It can weigh as much as one hundred pounds, and its long-legged, fluid stride carries it immense distances in search of prey. Wolves can run at a steady pace of fifteen miles an hour for many hours; sometimes they cover more than one hundred miles in a day. Sharp of eye and keen of hearing, wolves have powerful jaws, strong teeth and great resourcefulness in the hunt. They work in packs, isolating prey with deadly efficiency. All Europe knew them well once. Wolves ranged easily across the land, flourishing in the taiga – the vast belt of conifers stretching across the north of Russia – and in the dense forests of Germany and France. In those days, people would often hear the faint music of wolf howls floating in the air during the crepuscular hours. As long as food remained plentiful, wolves kept their distance from human settlements. But in the hungry months, when the winter nights drew in, they invaded the little towns near the forests. Silent as shadows, they nosed through the narrow streets, peering into windows and brushing against doors, alert for the scent and movement of the living. They wreaked havoc among the livestock, and they did not fear humanity. It was said that wolves invaded even the city of Paris during the brutal winter of 1450, slipping through a breach in the city walls and killing as many as forty citizens.

Death bringers, they were as feared as death itself. Wolves were said to be the souls of ancient savageries, so that in France, the twilight period when they sang was called "the time between the dog and the wolf" – the dog being the servant of humankind, and the wolf its master.

Inevitably, some humans sought to join the wolf in its mastery. If they succeeded, they became the werewolves of old, more vicious than wolves because they were charged with evil. They were secret enemies, who walked among humankind by day and sought its flesh by night.

Few mortals witnessed the transformation of a werewolf from human to beast shape or back. This was to be expected: Most men and women who could sink to the level of beasts guarded the secret carefully. Occasionally, however, someone saw the change and lived to tell about it.

Such an adventure befell a Roman slave named Niceros, who left his master's

*Before battle, warriors of Scandinavia donned great bearskins, thinking thus to gain ursine strength and courage that would enable them to overwhelm any foe.*

house one summer night for a tryst with a woman. It was a fine, balmy evening, and a jovial soldier whom he knew joined Niceros for his stroll. Together the two men walked along a road through olive groves, chatting comfortably of this and that. Their way passed a field of tombs, and Niceros' companion left him for a moment to stop among the whitened monuments. The slave turned his head away and studied the yellow moon riding the heavens. A harsh growl startled him, and he whirled.

Bathed in moonlight, the soldier stood stark naked among the stones. His tunic and sandals lay in a heap at his feet. Patches of hair on his body crawled outward along his flesh, turning to thick, lustrous fur. His hands writhed in the air, and the finger tips glittered and grew pointed. Then, with a harsh cough, he doubled over and dropped to the ground. After an instant, he raised his head and watched Niceros. The slave stared back, transfixed. The man he knew was gone. In his place, eyes gleaming gold, stood a wolf.

The beast did not attack. It raised its head and, from deep within its throat, produced a low note that wavered and climbed into a high, mournful howl. The noise rang among the marble stones. Then the wolf turned and, in great undulating strides, sped away among the olive trees.

Niceros took no chances. He bolted down the road, never halting until he arrived at the little farm where his paramour lived. The place was in an uproar when he arrived. A wolf had attacked the farmer's sheep. They lay in their byres,

their wool soaked with blood. Seeing this, Niceros stammered out his improbable tale. His mistress reassured him with wine and hearty words. It was an ordinary wolf, she said, and the farmer had driven the beast off himself, wounding it grievously with a sharpened stave.

But when Niceros returned to the city in the morning, he saw that he had not imagined the transformation in the field of tombs. He found his soldier friend dying of a stab wound received the night before — a wound whose origin he refused to explain even as his life slipped away.

If the soldier had escaped a violent end, he still would have found that gaining the freedom and the power of a beast carried a high price. The human who surrendered his humanity was lost, caught between the world of animals and men, gradually sinking deeper into savagery. In time, he became a stranger to even the humblest human pleasures — the shining faces of children, the taste of fresh-baked bread, the evenings of conversation by firelight. Gone were the gifts of learning and dreaming, gone the joy in honor and the delight in loveliness, gone the weeping and laughter. What he had left was a fugitive life — days of pretense, nights of lonely killing. It was said that a werewolf's howl was more mournful than that of a wild wolf because it was a lamentation.

The condition was accursed. In fact, the earliest legends of werewolves described people caught by imprecation, such as Lycaon, an ancient tyrant of Arcadia, in western Greece. This King, a hateful man, decided to test the perspicacity of Zeus by serving him a banquet of baked meats, some of which were human flesh. Outraged, the god transformed the tyrant into a wolf, dooming him always to be famished and to retain his human understanding of his plight. From the tale comes the term "lycanthrope," a word for "werewolf."

Sometimes the agent of the curse was human curiosity, the more laudable manifestation of Lycaon's arrogance. The poets of Scandinavia told a tale of this sort when they recited the adventures of two warriors of the mighty Volsung clan:

A chieftain named Sigmund once traveled on foot with his son Sinfjotli through the pine forests and along the dark fjords of the north. This was the summer when the older man gave the younger his final training for manhood; it was a season of long, light-filled days and the pleasures of the hunt.

Late one day, they came upon a hut of hide deep in the forest, the kind of place where outlaws dwelled. Sinfjotli drew back the flap that covered the door opening and peered into the hut. The little shelter was smoky and dim, but there was enough light to reveal the forms of two sleeping men and, hanging from the roof pole, two fine wolf pelts, the heads intact, the fangs gleaming white from gaping mouths. Quiet as a thief in the night, Sinfjotli slipped inside and took the pelts.

For a jest, he drew the larger pelt over his head and shoulders; the other he tossed to his father, who did the same. Then the two stared. They were mirror images of each other. Sigmund opened his mouth, and from it came a guttural bark;

his son pawed clumsily at the wolfskin, but it had closed about his body. Both then dropped to the ground. Where warriors had been, two wolves now paced.

Wolf instincts came easy. Together, they loped through the trees, pausing now and again to assess a scent. When they caught the smell of humans, they followed it until they came to a clearing where skin-clad hunters slept around a small campfire.

Sigmund and Sinfjotli hurtled out of the woods. Their jaws closed on the throats of the sleeping men. The hot, sweet-smelling human blood boiled up around them. In moments, the pair had burrowed their noses deep into the bodies, feeding on the flesh even before the victims had died. They fed in the manner of all wolves, gorging until their sides were swollen taut and they could eat no more; after all, they might not find flesh again for several days.

Sinfjotli at last flopped to the ground, panting. The wolf that was his father approached him, but such was the younger creature's frenzy that he took the movement for a threat. He leaped to his feet, stiff-legged, his hackles rising, and he snarled. Confused, the older wolf lurched forward and buried his teeth in Sinfjotli's throat. Sinfjotli fell bleeding at his father's feet. Then, as if dim memories of his humanity stirred, the older wolf lay down beside the younger, whining and licking the jagged wound he had made.

For hours, the two animals remained among the human men they had slaughtered. Finally, for reasons no one could ever explain, the power of the spell waned, and the wolf pelts loosened from the human frames. Father and wounded son stood upright and surveyed the carnage. Sadly, without speaking, they kindled a fire and burned the wolfskins that had robbed them of humanity, and they went forward to their human ventures.

Few mortals ever escaped the coils of bestiality once they were enmeshed. What so often made their fate more tragic was that they had not sought a beast's power in the first place.

There seemed to be a certain caprice and cruelty in this, as if pockets of evil power existed everywhere to trap unwary mortals. Thus, in Italy, those who chanced to sleep outdoors on a Friday night when a full moon might shine on their faces were said to be doomed to a werewolf's fate, as were shepherds who drank from streams that had been visited earlier by wolves. In some lands, fate was thought to be determined by birth: Germans believed that the seventh of seven consecutive daughters carried the werewolf stain. In the Balkans, those who plucked and wore a rare white marsh flower were doomed. (That flower's name has been lost.) And in a few countries, children born at Christmas were said to be at risk, perhaps because Christmas fell near the winter solstice, when evil walked abroad, or perhaps because the night was sacred to the birth of Christ.

These people were victims of an evil they could not understand, and many of them took no pleasure in the savagery forced upon them. Some werewolves fought against their instincts and hunted other living things only when they were forced to by starvation. Some learned to detect the signs that foreshadowed their transformations, which might occur every night at dusk, or every night of the full moon or even only once a year. Such people prepared secret chambers in their houses and locked themselves in when the time approached. Typically, the rooms were situated in remote corners of the house, where howling would be muffled, and were provided with intricate systems of locks and bolts that confounded the beast's simple wit. (The locks were easily managed when the bestial state receded.)

In a few instances, protective arrangements of this kind were public knowledge. This was the situation some centuries ago in the Lombardy region of Italy, in a tidy, pious village called St. Angelo.

That village's grappling with the werewolf curse began one Christmas Eve, when the *presepio* – the painted nativity scene of the region – shone in the candlelit church. Cheerful fires burned in every house, and the scent of baking – of raisin-studded Christmas cakes and of the little hat-shaped pastries called *cappelletti* – hovered in the narrow streets. During those joyful hours, a boy was born to a couple of the village, but this was no holy child. Because of the timing of his birth, he was destined to be a werewolf, and all the villagers knew it.

They were a strong and close-knit people, however, and they gathered around the little family. The boy was allowed to live in peace. He showed a peculiarly sweet and gentle nature, which became more marked as he grew. He played with the other village children in the shade of

*It was told of men of the Volsung clan that they unwittingly brought tragedy upon themselves when, in jest, they covered their bodies with wolfskins. The wolfishness entered their souls, turning son against father and father against son.*

## A sly killer

All children know the tale of Red Riding Hood and her miraculous escape from a wolf. The children of earlier centuries, however, heard a more somber version:

In Germany, winter was a lean season when hollow-bellied wolves prowled near human paths. But the creature Red Riding Hood met was more than a wolf. He surely had once been a man: He knew the ways of men and the naïveté of little girls.

When he spied the bright-cloaked figure trotting along the forest track, he might have sprung, but there were other mortals about. Instead, he called out softly from the underbrush, "Where do you go, my pretty maid?"

Seeing the silvery, doglike face that peered from the brambles, Red Riding Hood smiled, delighted by the talking animal.

"To my grandmother's house, dog," she replied. "The house at the end of this track."

At once, the wolf conceived a plan. With a flick of his tail, he vanished, speeding ahead to the little cottage. There he dispatched the grandmother without much interest: She was old and dry. Then he climbed into her comfortable bed to wait.

After a few moments, the child knocked at the door. "Come in," the wolf fluted.

The child entered, but paused out of range. He peered over the covers.

"Why grandmother, what big ears you have," she said.

"The better to hear you, my dear."

She came closer. "Why grandmother, what big eyes you have."

"The better to see you, my dear."

She stepped closer still. "Grandmother, what big teeth you have."

"The better to eat you with."

Terrified, she whirled to run, but the wolf was quick, and his teeth met in the red cloak in an instant. Then he feasted slowly and pleasurably on the rosy flesh and sweet young blood of Red Riding Hood. What he could not eat he carried away in chunks and buried for a later meal.

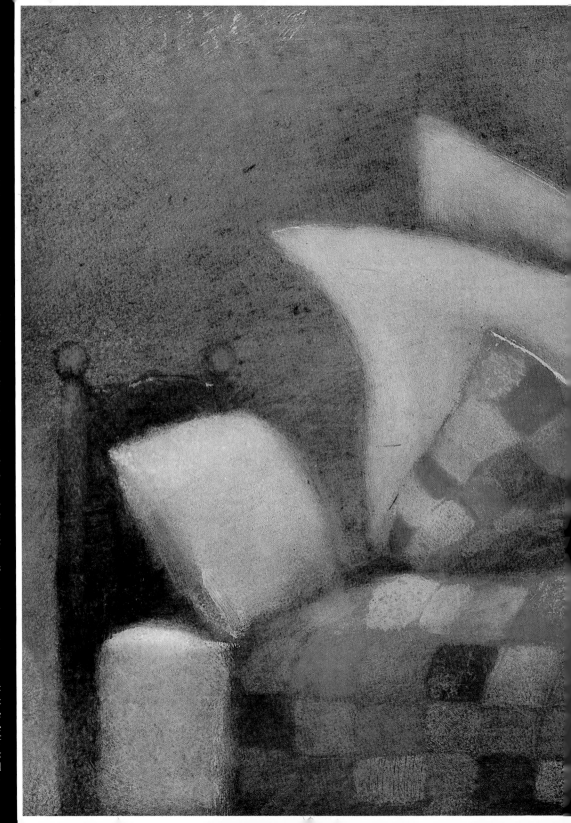

*Nights spent prowling in animal form doomed humans to ultimate grief. So a werewolf of Italy, although he tried to forfend it, slaughtered and fed upon his own wife.*

the tall poplars of the town; he herded goats and cattle in the pastures along the banks of the Po River; he learned the crafts of the wine maker and the cheese maker.

On one night each year, however, when the bells tolled for the Christmas Eve Mass, the curse came upon him. At the first sound of ringing, he tore at his clothes. Screaming, he dropped to his hands and knees. He writhed in the dirt of the village streets, gasping and foaming at the mouth, and as he writhed, his body lengthened and changed. When he rose again, he rose in the form of a wolf. Yellow eyes glittering, fanged mouth slavering,

he launched himself at parents and neighbors alike. When he was small, the people of St. Angelo tried to restrain him; as he grew older, they fended him off with sticks, although they took care not to harm him. Eventually, they knew, he would turn from them and race into the darkened fields, and no more would be seen of him until morning. The villagers let him go. They locked their livestock away, but they prayed for the boy's soul.

When Christmas Day dawned, the youth always returned, wan and tired and bloodstained. He would sleep through the day and then resume his normal life. His

neighbors treated him as one of their own. And their daughters admired him. In his twenty-third year, he married a farmer's pretty daughter, whom he had known all his life, and set up his own household, as other young men of the village did.

The two made a happy pair—and a sensible one. With care, they planned for the young husband's affliction. Each Christmas Eve before midnight, they agreed, the wife would send her husband out. She would lock their goats in the small shed that leaned against the house; she would seal herself in the house. All night she would watch, and she would not open the door in any circumstance, until she heard three loud raps on it. These would signify that her husband had regained his human form, that the blood lust had left him and he would do her no harm.

So they lived contentedly for several years. Each Christmas Eve, the wife bade her husband leave before his sickness came upon him. Each year she waited through the night while the thing he had become scratched and whined and howled in the dark. Dawn always brought the three required raps. At the third, she opened the door to let her naked, ashen-faced husband in. She sponged the blood from his body and then put him gently in their bed.

Their life might have continued this way except for the wife's error. It happened in a year when she was heavy and drowsy with her first child. As she had before, she sent her husband away on Christmas Eve, settling by the fire to rest. In the small hours, however, she apparently thought she heard the knocking of her husband. (This the villagers later surmised, since she had clearly unlocked and unbolted the door at some point and thrown it open to the night.)

The villagers went to the little house on Christmas morning with the woman's husband, whom they found lurching naked through the streets, weeping and muttering to himself. His lips were cracked and crusted with blood; his hair was stiffly peaked with it. Displaying their custom-

## A secret life unmasked

Although the body of a werebeast changed its outward shape, it remained the same body, housing the same spirit. Thus, a wound received by a werebeast in its animal guise was inevitably transferred to its human form. A tale from France provides a case in point.

Near Riom, in the Auvergne, where the landscape was a tumbled tableau of rocky pinnacles and heavy forest, lived a lord who sent his master huntsman in search of a wolf that had been attacking his flocks. The huntsman found the animal one day at dusk in a wood near the manor pastures; he drove it into the underbrush, and there the creature turned on him.

Its spring knocked him to the ground, but the man was quick to recover. He drew his hunting knife and severed one of the beast's forepaws. With a howl, the wolf leaped away and vanished into the wood.

The hunter took the paw for his trophy, placing it in a box and presenting it at once to his master with pride. But when the casket was opened, it did not contain a paw. In the box was a woman's hand adorned with a ring that was the twin of the lord's own signet.

Both men knew what this meant: The hand was that of the lord's wife. The lord strode to her chambers. He found, as he expected, that physicians were attending her there, dealing with the consequences of what she claimed was an accident: Her left hand had been severed at the wrist. "Here is your hand, woman," he said. And he ordered her burned at the stake for being a werewolf.

ary gentleness, the village folk covered him with a blanket and led him home.

They found a nightmare. The door of the little house stood open, and the interior was cold and sour-smelling. The ashes of the fire, scattered everywhere, cast a pall on the once-gleaming table and the empty cradle that stood beside the hearth, on the shards of pottery that littered the floor, and on the body of the young wife, torn and chewed beyond recognition.

The villagers did what they could. They buried the remains of the wife and the infant she had carried. They kept watch on the husband, but they withdrew from him and from the evil that lived in him. And they did not watch him closely enough. One day not long afterward, unable to live with the knowledge of what he was and what he had done, he stabbed himself and surrendered to eternal darkness.

An untimely death thus ended what an untimely birth had begun. In truth, the villagers of St. Angelo, tolerant as they had been, spoke only relief at the demise of the youth who had walked among them as a brother. They had seen what his werewolf's teeth could do and had shuddered at the cold miasma of the curse that circumscribed his life.

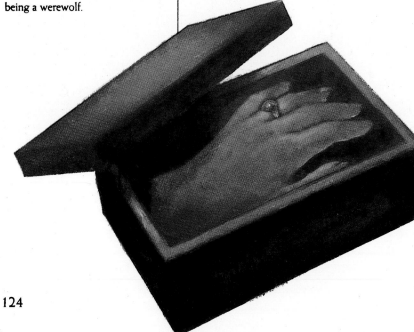

Their reaction was not surprising in that fear-filled age – or any age. For the most part, those known to be werewolves, no matter how kind they might be in human form, were persecuted by their fellows.

Such was the case in Brittany, for instance, where troubadours long sang the lay of *bisclavaret*, or "werewolf." It told of a young baron who had been placed under an enchantment, from what source none could tell. Three nights out of every seven, this man wandered alone into the forests that covered his lands. Driven by a terrible compulsion, he shed his clothes, which were all that helped him retain his human form, and hunted forest animals until morning, when he dressed again and became once more a man.

The baron had a wife. The beginning of the marriage had been happy; it might have continued so. But the wife, jealous of his absences, wheedled her husband's secret from him. The knowledge changed her. Instead of the man, she saw only the beast that lurked within him, and the old magic filled her with disgust.

Unmoved by his pain, she consoled herself by taking a lover, and at length she arranged for freedom from the husband who now was loathsome to her. She followed the baron into the forest and stole the clothes that he discarded there, so that she might live with her paramour.

Condemned to a beast's existence, the baron pined. He could not speak, but his bestial instincts left him, and eventually – and humiliatingly – he became a kind of pet to the Breton King. In the end, sang the troubadours, the wife's betrayal was discovered. The baron was restored to his human form, and his wife went into exile.

The Breton tale was a slight one, but emblematic of the hatred most humans felt for those isolated by evil magic. In many countries, it was thought that the only proper end for werebeasts, no matter what the cause of their condition, was slaughter. Even though some people feared that the creatures could return from the grave as vampires, they were hunted as mercilessly as wild wolves, or indeed, as anything that differed from the norm.

But there remained folk who believed that the curse could be broken by measures that fell short of killing — measures that required steadfast courage on the part of the men and women who had to face werewolves in their bestial form. It was thought that if a human looked directly at the beast and uttered the simple accusation, "You are a werewolf," or addressed the creature three times by its given human name, the animal nature would fall away at once. It was also said that the curse would be lifted if a mortal pricked the skull of the werebeast, drawing three drops of blood. Such an injury would soon heal, and the graver affliction — the blighted human spirit — would be cured forever.

Tactics of this kind demanded more than simple courage. They required that men and women have a generosity of spirit and a love of their fellows strong enough to overcome the revulsion that murdersome beasts engendered. A French tale showed what human compassion might do in the face of the creatures of darkness.

That tale begins with a father's betrayal of his daughter. The details of the deed are less important than its consequences, but in brief, it happened this way: The man was a merchant who had fallen on hard times; in his travels he had crossed the magical boundaries of a beast's territory and thereby entered its power; he angered it and, by the rules of the place, was forced to forfeit either his own life or that of his daughter, whom he dearly loved. He called her his Beauty. But his love did not outweigh his fear of death. And so — weeping for her fate, as the storytellers were fond of saying — he returned home and told her that she must be sacrificed.

On an afternoon in January, after a day's ride through bare, black-branched forests under a lowering sky, he left the maiden, as he had been instructed, at a stone bridge by the dark waters of a certain lake and rode away, a free man.

The Beauty stood for some moments where she had been set down. Before her, the bridge stretched across the lake to the deep gates of a castle. At her back, the forest branches hissed and shuffled in the wind.

She had no choice: She must go forward. The moment she set foot on the bridge, the massive doors at the far end swung open, but she could not see what lay within the castle, for the arched portal was filled with smoky shadow. Across the bridge and through the archway she walked, passing into the daylight again.

Yet this was a different daylight. Above the castle walls, now golden in sunlight, soared a blue vault of sky, fretted with

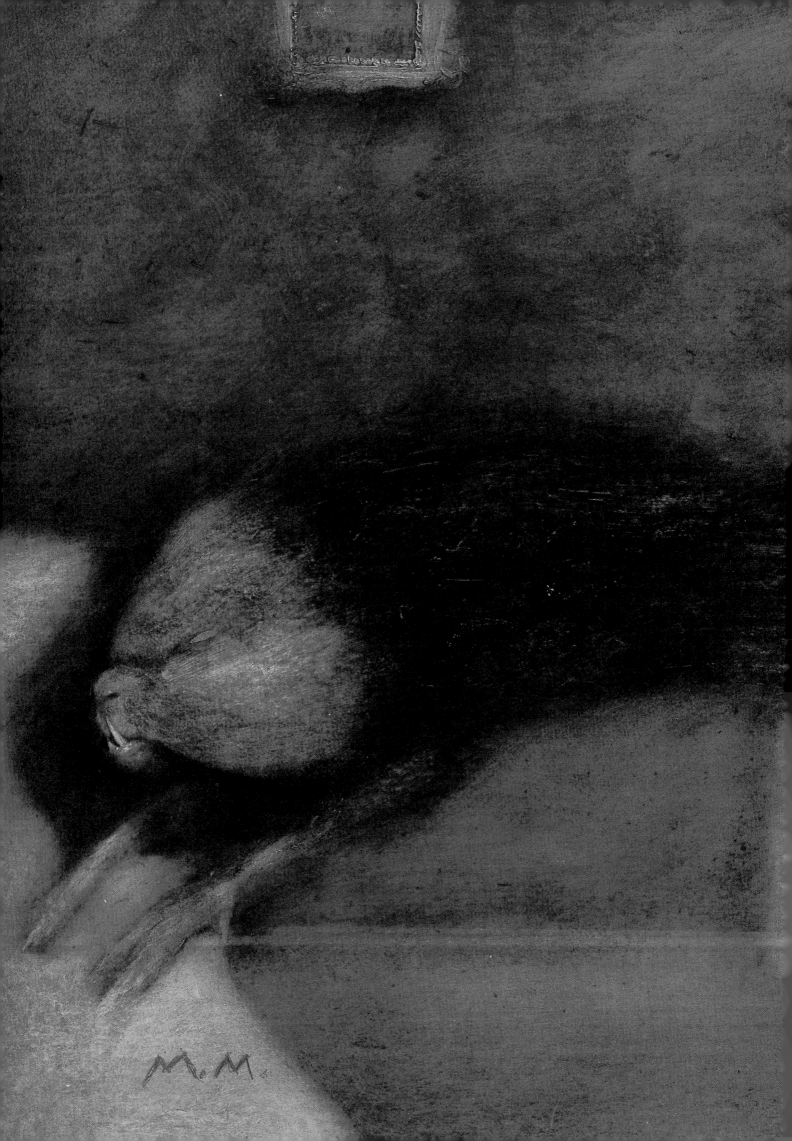

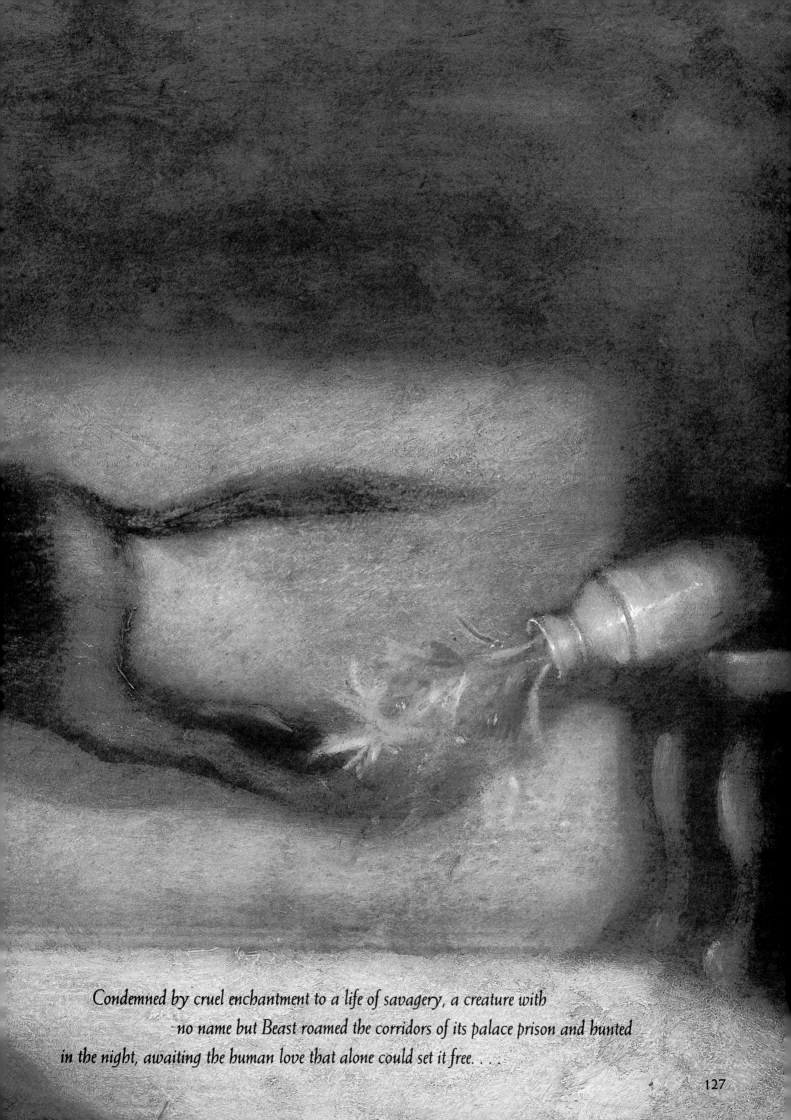

Condemned by cruel enchantment to a life of savagery, a creature with
no name but Beast roamed the corridors of its palace prison and hunted
in the night, awaiting the human love that alone could set it free. . . .

*... Bereft of love, the Beast despaired and gave itself to death. Yet life was offered at the last, from the heart of a maiden called Beauty.*

dancing, lamblike clouds. Below it spread a garden, a mosaic defined by green scrolls of box and pyramids of red-berried holly, and brightened by the flowers of every season—snowdrop and crocus, tulip and iris, heavy-headed peony and white-winged columbine. The garden made a carpet for a towering house that rose in its center, regarding the Beauty from hundreds of windows.

Reluctant to enter the dwelling, she threw back the hood of her cloak and paced the pleached garden walks, looking for signs of her captor. But there was no sign. The garden was quiet, and the air still and thick with the scents of flowers. At length, the light began to fade. A chill settled on the garden. Straightening her back, the Beauty left the garden and approached the house: She had no desire to meet its owner in a darkened courtyard.

The doors stood open, and as she passed through them into a white-walled hall, a faint cascade of bells sounded. In a great hearth at the end of the hall, a fire leaped into life. Around the walls, candle flames grew and glowed.

Emboldened, the Beauty began to explore. She saw no sign of any life, but everywhere she walked, unliving things awakened, not only candles to light her way, but doors that opened invitingly into tapestried rooms and shutters that swung wide to reveal changing vistas of the moonlit gardens. She found a chamber marked with her own name and filled with treasures that made her smile—a crystal chess set whose chessmen bowed politely to her; an inlaid lute that sounded a sweet chord when she looked upon it; a silver basin and ewer busily exuding clouds of fragrant steam; a wardrobe whose doors opened up to offer a rainbow of

dresses that rustled coyly at her glance; a pretty bed hung in white. Near the bed stood a table laid with cups of silver and dishes of gold. The Beauty peered more closely at it, and the smile left her face. The table was laid for two.

Then she sighed and set to work, adorning herself for sacrifice. With help from officious linens and the somewhat nervous ewer, she bathed. After what appeared to be a dispute among the contents of the wardrobe, she dressed. Finally, rustling in silks, she went to the table to await the creature her father had given her to.

An hour passed while the Beauty sat motionless, ignoring the wine cups that slid hopefully toward her hand. Then from the corridor came a sound—a rhythmic clicking that halted by the door. It opened, and she stood up to face what must appear. A bestial shape huddled low at the entrance to the chamber. Pawing clumsily at the doorpost, it reared to its hind feet and shuffled into the room, bringing with it a foul scent of ammonia and musk. After one glance at the thing —a flashing glance that showed a heavy head bent down by curving tusks and long legs terminating in claws—the maiden bowed her head. But the Beast did not spring. It spoke.

The words were indistinct, coming as they did from a mouth not shaped for speaking. Still, she could understand them, and she detected the bitterness in the voice.

"My dear, do you like what you see?" said the Beast.

She swayed, and at once the Beast said softly, "I will not harm you. I will not touch you, unless you give me leave. Only let me sit with you a while."

Then the Beauty nodded. She sank into her chair again. She did not look as the Beast crawled into its chair, but from the corner of her eye she could see that a raw mound of scarlet flesh and white bone appeared on its plate. The Beast lowered its head to eat. Breathing heavily, it crunched and snuffled and lapped, while she regarded her own golden plate. A fine little fowl and creamy sauces had materialized on it, but she had no appetite.

Yet she was surprised that first evening. When the Beast had fed, it drew away from her so that she could no longer catch its scent. It began to speak, and so calm and charming was its conversation that she was drawn to reply, stiffly at first and then with ease. She even laughed, and at that sound the Beast paused. After a moment's silence, it said heavily, "I am bound to ask: Will you marry me?" The Beauty shook her head and then, trembling, clasped her arms across her breast. The creature made no move in her direction, however; it sat absolutely still in the manner of a frightened animal. The Beauty looked, then, and saw the Beast's velvet eyes, fringed with dark lashes like a man's and glistening with tears.

It turned away from her and shambled from the room, dropping to all fours when it reached the door. It vanished into the corridor, and the door closed behind it. In the room, the candles flickered and died; the dishes on the table disappeared; and with a sullen snap, the bed curtains opened, commanding her to sleep.

During the night, the Beast's claws clicked up and down the corridor outside the room. Later, she heard a door slam far below and, later still, a high-pitched squeal – the death cry of some small animal in the garden. But that was all.

She did not see the Beast again until the following evening, when it returned to her chamber. As before, it talked with her and pleased her with its talk. As before, it asked for her hand and, when she refused, quietly left her. And so the days passed. Whatever the Beauty wished for, she had: books to read, the lute to play, the garden to walk in.

Each night the Beast came to her. Delicate of sensibility, it no longer fed in her presence, but it amused and taught her with its talk, and she grew to feel comfortable in its presence. After a time, she allowed it to lie at her feet by the hearth, and one night, much to her own surprise, she reached to stroke the shining fur on the Beast's back.

"You are what the courtiers call *beau laid*. You are 'beautiful ugly,' " she said.

Under the Beauty's caressing hand, the Beast remained profoundly still. Then it asked the question it asked each night: "Will you marry me?"

And as she did each night, the Beauty refused. But later, when she lay in the dark and heard it pacing, her eyes pricked her with bewildering pain.

Shortly after this, disturbed in her heart, the Beauty asked to return to her father. Her captor refused, but she asked again each night, putting her question with the same regularity as the Beast put its own. At last it said dully, "I shall die if you leave me and do not return."

She promised to return, if she were allowed to walk among her own kind once more. The Beast then agreed to let her go – for one month only.

She left the next morning, riding a horse that appeared on the bridge. A mule appeared, too, and it was heavily laden with packs of golden coins.

"Blood money," said her father grimly, when he had welcomed her. But he took the money all the same.

It was not long before the Beauty settled into the routine of her own house, filled as it was with human business and human chatter. She let the month slip by and stayed a day longer, and then another day. But on the night of that day, terrible images swam into her dreams. Voices called to her from the depths of sleep, and one of them was her own voice, repeating the promise that she had given.

She awoke in darkness and rose at once. Taking one of her father's horses, she set off through the woods again. They were dark and deep; the journey was slow; and the branches, full of leaves now, tore at her hair and cloak. Late in the morning, she reached the lake. She set the horse at a trot across the stone bridge that led to the Beast's castle.

The gates were closed. She called a command, but they did not move.

Stricken with fright and other feelings she could not define, the Beauty dismounted and slapped the horse to send it home. With all her strength, she pressed against the heavy doors. At last, issuing a reluctant groan, they opened enough to let her into the garden.

The garden was dead, an ugly tangle of withered vines and brown hedges and dry, drifting leaves. She ran through the house, calling, but no voice replied. The hall was still and shadowed, full of dust. She called for light, but no candle leaped into flame for her.

The Beauty searched the Beast's house with the urgency of fear. Then she rushed out to the great garden. There, lying in the dirt, she found the Beast, dead or dying. Its fur was matted and thick with brambles, and its eyes stared dully at the sky. She flung herself down beside it, threw her arms around its neck and wept at having broken her promise. Then she saw the Beast's eyes flicker—the shining of a soul in the animal body.

The Beast gazed upon her, and she said "Yes" and "Yes" again.

The silver cascade of bells sounded as they had sounded many months before. A wind sprang up and blew a wave of leaves into the air. They fell and shrouded the Beast where it lay.

Hastily she brushed them away. The Beast was no longer there. She bowed her head, tears dropping onto the ground where the Beast had lain.

When she looked up again, she found that a man stood before her, a tall man clad in velvet and boots of Spanish leather. His voice, when he spoke, was one she knew.

"My dear," he said with a twinkle in his eyes, "do you like what you see?"

So the old tale ended with the release of the young lord from his bestial prison and his union with the woman who had freed him. The storytellers differed as to what had cast him into the enchantment and bound him in his castle. Some said his parents had been cursed, some that a sorceress had enspelled him and forced him to become a servant of the night until such time as a human woman willingly gave herself to him. But this much was agreed: The magic that had bound him could not match the human love and courage that set him free.

Indeed, humanity always was the last defense against the spells of darkness and unreason. Human courage fought night's creatures back. Human love and loyalty kept them at bay.

And as the strength of humankind began to grow, the ancient demons of night began to dwindle. Their memories lingered on, in old tales and nightmares, in the fears of death, in random hauntings. These were mere tatters of the fabric of an elder world, however, frail descendants, all, of the gods of darkness who once held the world in thrall.

# The Fox Maiden

Silky-furred, bright-eyed, wily and sweetly mocking, the little *kitsune* – foxes – of Japan were both loved and feared by mortals. Some *kitsune* served the harvest god, and these were honored: At the god's shady roadside shrines and in his mighty temple compounds stood hosts of pretty foxes carved in stone and adorned with jeweled eyes. But most *kitsune* were evil beasts that could assume the shape of beautiful women and rob mortal men of vigor and goodness.

Among such malevolent *kitsune*, the most powerful and enduring was Tamamo no Maé. In her human guise, she was a courtesan so exquisite and skilled that she was called the Jewel Maiden. Her victims were kings and emperors.

Tamamo's origins were obscure. It was thought that, thousands of years before she arrived in Japan, she had been an Indian King's con-

sort, appearing at times as a woman and at times as a white fox with nine tails. As either, she was heartless: Her chief pleasure was the slaughter of innocents. Eventually, she was expelled from India.

Legend said that the fox-woman next appeared in China, in the harem of the Shang tyrant Chou Hsin. To satisfy her extravagant tastes, the besotted Emperor created vast pleasure gardens whose lakes were filled with wine and whose trees were hung with baskets of delicacies. Knowing that she would appreciate a fillip of humiliation, he commanded the ladies of his court to dance nude among the flowers of these gardens for her amusement. They refused. So Chou Hsin devised a better entertainment: He forced the women into a pit filled with vipers and bees. As Tamamo remarked in her soft voice, the ladies danced quite

briskly then. They died in agony.

The dissipation of the Chinese court became so constant and egregious that the people at last revolted against the scandal. Tamamo was executed and her body burned. But from the ashes sprang a snowy fox. Swift as the wind, it made for Japan.

In the Court of the Rising Sun, Tamamo took woman's form again and seduced Toba, Emperor of Japan. He steadily weakened in her company. Finally, during a night of storms, he fell into a swoon, calling her name. At that, a nimbus of triumphant light played around Tamamo's head. The Emperor's counselors saw it and recognized what she must be. They exposed Tamamo's nature by holding a mirror before her face. The glass reflected not the countenance of a woman, but the white-furred muzzle of a fox.

By this, the evil magic was broken. The woman reverted to fox form and streaked away among the pavilions of the palace. For some days, the creature lingered near, killing small animals and birds when it could, until the people set their dogs on it.

The fox then fled, retreating to the sulfur-smoking moor of Nasu, in the central part of the island of Honshu, where the owls sang all night long in mournful chorus and the jackals whined on the wind. There, the *kitsune* dwindled to a stone, it was said, and lay solitary in sullen grandeur on the plain. Nothing that touched the stone or even approached it survived the experience. It cast a miasma so venomous that insects and birds littered the ground nearby. Poets said only clouds could fly over Sessho-Seki, a name that meant the "Stone of Life Destruction."

# Picture Credits

*The sources for the illustrations in this book are shown below. When it is known, the name of the artist precedes the source of the picture.*

Cover: Artwork by Matt Mahurin. 1-5: Artwork by John Collier. 6-11: Artwork by John Howe. 12, 13: Artwork by John Collier. 14: Artwork by Matt Mahurin. 16, 17: Artwork by John Jude Palencar. 18, 19: Artwork by Marshall Arisman. 23: Artwork by Matt Mahurin. 24, 25: Artwork by Marshall Arisman. 26, 27: Artwork by Matt Mahurin. 28, 29: Artwork by John Howe. 30- 37: Artwork by Marshall Arisman. 38, 39: Artwork by Kunio Hagio. 42, 43: Artwork by Matt Mahurin. 44, 45: Artwork by Michael Paraskevas. 47-50: Artwork by Brian McCall. 52, 53: Henry Fuseli, courtesy The Detroit Institute of Arts, gift of Mr. and Mrs. Bert L. Smokler and Mr. and Mrs. Lawrence A. Fleischman. 54, 55: Artwork by Gary Kelley. 57: Artwork by John Jude Palencar. 58, 59: Artwork by John Collier. 62-71: Artwork by Willi Glasauer. 72-77: Artwork by Yvonne Gilbert. 79: Artwork by Michael Paraskevas. 80, 81: Artwork by Kunio Hagio. 82, 83: Artwork by Matt Mahurin. 84: Artwork by Sam Bayer. 86: Artwork by Marshall Arisman. 88, 89: Artwork by Michael Paraskevas. 91: Artwork by Matt Mahurin. 92-97: Artwork by Gary Kelley. 98-107: Artwork by Mark Langeneckert. 108-113: Artwork by Matt Mahurin. 114, 115: Artwork by Marshall Arisman. 118, 119: Artwork by Michael Paraskevas. 120, 121: Artwork by Matt Mahurin. 122, 123: Artwork by Marshall Arisman. 124: Artwork by Sam Bayer. 126-129: Artwork by Matt Mahurin. 132-139: Artwork by John Howe. 144: Artwork by John Collier.

# Bibliography

Aldington, Richard, and Delano Ames, transls. *New Larousse Encyclopedia of Mythology*. London: The Hamlyn Publishing Group, 1974.*

Aylesworth, Thomas G.:
*The Story of Vampires*. New York: McGraw-Hill, 1977.
*The Story of Werewolves*. New York: McGraw-Hill, 1978.
*Vampires and Other Ghosts*. Reading, Massachusetts: Addison-Wesley, 1972.
*Werewolves and Other Monsters*. Reading, Massachusetts: Addison-Wesley, 1971.*

Baring-Gould, Sabine, *The Book of Were-Wolves: Being an Account of a Terrible Superstition*. Detroit: Gale Research, no date.*

Berenstain, Michael, *Troll Book*. New York: Random House, 1980.*

Black, G. F., compiler, *County Folk-Lore: Examples of Printed Folk-Lore Concerning the Orkney & Shetland Islands*. Ed. by Northcote W. Thomas. Vol. 3. London: David Nutt for The Folk-Lore Society, 1903.

Brasch, Rudolph, *The Supernatural and You!* Stanmore, Australia: Cassell Australia Limited, 1976.

Briggs, Katharine:
*Abbey Lubbers, Banshees & Boggarts: An Illustrated Encyclopedia of Fairies*. New York: Pantheon Books, 1979.*
*British Folktales*. New York: Pantheon Books, 1977.
*A Dictionary of British Folk-Tales in the English Language*. 2 vols. London: Routledge & Kegan Paul, 1971.
*An Encyclopedia of Fairies: Hobgoblins, Brownies, Bogies, and Other Supernatural Creatures*. New York: Pantheon Books, 1976.*

Bringsværd, Tor Åge, *Phantoms and Fairies from Norwegian Folklore*. Transl. by Pat Shaw Iversen. Oslo: Johan Grundt Tanum Forlag, no date.

Cavendish, Richard, ed., *Man, Myth & Magic*. 11 vols. New York: Marshall Cavendish, 1983.*

Chickering, Howell D., Jr., transl., *Beowulf: A Dual-Language Edition*. New York: Anchor Books, 1977.*

Child, Francis James, ed., *The English and Scottish Popular Ballads*, Vol. 5. New York: Cooper Square, 1962.*

Cohen, Daniel, *A Natural History of Unnatural Things*. New York: McCall, 1971.*

Cole, Joanna, compiler, *Best-Loved Folktales of the World*. New York: Doubleday, 1982.*

Copper, Basil, *The Vampire in Legend, Fact and Art*. London: Robert Hale, 1973.*

Daniels, Cora Linn, and C. M. Stevans, eds., *Encyclopaedia of Superstitions, Folklore, and the Occult Sciences of the World*. Vols. 1 and 2. Detroit: Gale Research, 1971 (reprint of 1903 edition).*

Davidson, Hilda R., *Gods and Myths of Northern Europe*. New York: Penguin Books, 1982.

Davis, F. Hadland, *Myths & Legends of Japan*. London: George G. Harrap, 1912.

Dégh, Linda, ed., *Folktales of Hungary*. Transl. by Judit Halász. Chicago: The University of Chicago Press, 1965.

De Givry, Grillot, *Witchcraft, Magic & Alchemy*. Transl. by J. Courtenay Locke. New York: Dover Publications, 1971 (reprint of 1931 edition).

Dömötör, Tekla, *Hungarian Folk Beliefs*. Transl. by Christopher M. Hann. Bloomington: Indiana University Press, 1982.

Edwards, Gillian, *Hobgoblin and Sweet Puck: Fairy Names and Natures*. London: Geoffrey Bles, 1974.

Emerson, Oliver Farrar, "The Earliest English Translations of Bürger's Lenore." Cleveland: Western Reserve University Press, Bulletin No. 3, May 1915.*

Farson, Daniel, *Vampires, Zombies, and Monster Men*. Garden City, New York: Doubleday, 1976.

*Folklore, Myths and Legends of Britain*. London: The Reader's Digest Association, 1973.

Garden, Nancy, *Werewolves*. Philadelphia: J. B. Lippincott, 1973.*

Grimm, Jacob, *Teutonic Mythology*. 4 vols. Transl. by James Steven Stallybrass. Gloucester, Massachusetts: Peter Smith, 1976 (reprints of 1883 and 1888 editions).

Grimm, Jakob Ludwig Karl, and Wilhelm Karl Grimm, *The German Legends of the Brothers Grimm*. 2 vols. Ed. and transl. by Donald Ward. Philadelphia, Pennsylvania: Institute for the Study of Human Issues, 1981.

Hamel, Frank, *Human Animals: Werewolves & Other Transformations*. New Hyde Park, New York: University Books, 1969 (reprint of 1915 edition).

Hartland, Edwin Sidney, *The Science of Fairy Tales: An Inquiry into Fairy Mythology*. Detroit: Singing Tree Press, 1968 (reprint of 1891 edition).

Haskins, Jim, *Werewolves*. New York: Franklin Watts, 1981.*

Hastings, James, ed., *Confirmation – Drama*. Vol. 4 of *Encyclopaedia of Religion and Ethics*. New York: Charles Scribner's Sons, 1928.*

Hearn, Lafcadio, *Glimpses of Unfamiliar Japan*. Vol. 1. Boston: Houghton Mifflin, 1894.

Henderson, William, *Notes on the Folk-Lore of the Northern Counties of England and the Borders*. London: W. Satchell, Peyton, 1879.*

Hill, Douglas, and Pat Williams, *The Supernatural*. London: Aldus Books, 1965.

Holmberg, Uno, *Finno-Ugric, Siberian*. Vol. 4 of *The Mythology of All Races*. Ed. by John Arnott MacCulloch. New York: Cooper Square, 1964.

Hoyt, Olga, *Lust for Blood: The Consuming Story of Vampires*. New York: Stein and Day, 1984.*

Hurwood, Bernhardt J.:
*Passport to the Supernatural: An Occult Compendium from All Ages and Many Lands*. New York: Taplinger, 1972.*
*Vampires*. New York: Quick Fox, 1981.*

Hyatt, Victoria, and Joseph W. Charles, *The Book of Demons*. London: Lorrimer, 1974.

James, Grace, *Green Willow and Other Japanese Fairy Tales*. London: Macmillan, 1912.*

Jones, Ernest, *On the Nightmare*. London: Leonard & Virginia Woolf, 1931.

Jones, Louis C., "Italian Werewolves." *New York Folklore Quarterly*, Autumn 1950.*

Katzeff, Paul, *Full Moons*. Secaucus, New Jersey: Citadel Press, 1981.

Kiessling, Nicolas, *The Incubus in English Literature: Provenance and Progeny*. Pullman: Washington State University Press, 1977.

Kittredge, George Lyman, *Witchcraft in Old and New England*. New York: Russell & Russell, 1956.

Kriss, Marika, *Werewolves, Shapeshifters, & Skinwalkers*. Los Angeles: Sherbourne Press, 1972.*

Lawson, John Cuthbert, *Modern Greek Folklore and Ancient Greek Religion: A Study in Survivals*. New Hyde Park, New York: University Books, 1964.*

Leach, Maria, ed., *Funk & Wagnall's Standard Dictionary of Folklore, Mythology and Legend*. 2 vols. New York: Funk & Wagnalls, 1949.*

Lopez, Barry Holstun, *Of Wolves and Men*. New York: Charles Scribner's Sons, 1978.*

MacCulloch, John Arnott, *Eddic*. Vol. 2 of *The Mythology of All Races*. New York: Cooper Square, 1964.

MacCulloch, John Arnott, and Jan Machal, *Celtic, Slavic*. Vol. 3 of *The Mythology of All Races*. New York: Cooper Square, 1964.

McHargue, Georgess:
*Meet the Vampire*. New York: J. B. Lippincott, 1979.*
*Meet the Werewolf*. New York: J. B. Lippincott, 1976.*

McNally, Raymond T., *A Clutch of Vampires*. Greenwich, Connecticut: New York Graphic Society, 1974.

Magnússon, Eiríkr, and William Morris, transls., *The Story of Grettir the Strong*. London: George Prior, 1980 (reprint of 1869 edition).*

Mason, Eugene, transl., *French Mediaeval Romances from the Lays of Marie de France*. London: J. M. Dent & Sons, 1976 (reprint of 1924 edition).*

Masters, Anthony, *The Natural History of the Vampire*. New York: G. P. Putnam's Sons, 1972.*

Newall, Venetia, *The Encyclopedia of Witchcraft & Magic*. New York: The Dial Press, 1974.

O'Donnell, Elliott, *Werwolves*. New York: Longvue Press, 1965.*

Ozaki, Yei Theodora, *Warriors of Old Japan and Other Stories*. Boston: Houghton Mifflin, 1909.*

Perkowski, Jan L., *Vampires of the Slavs*. Cambridge, Massachusetts: Slavica Publishers, 1976.

Radford, Edwin, and M. A. Radford, *Encyclopaedia of Superstitions*. Westport, Connecticut: Greenwood Press, 1969.

Ralston, William R. S., *The Songs of*

the Russian People, as Illustrative of Slavonic Mythology and Russian Social Life. New York: Haskell House Publishers, 1970 (reprint of 1872 edition).*

Robinson, B. W., Kuniyoshi: The Warrior-Prints. Ithaca, New York: Cornell University Press, 1982.

Rolleston, T. W., The High Deeds of Finn and Other Bardic Romances of Ancient Ireland. New York: Lemma Publishing, 1973.*

Ronay, Gabriel, The Dracula Myth. London: W. H. Allen, 1972.

Schlauch, Margaret, transl., The Saga of the Volsungs: The Saga of Ragnar Lodbrok, together with the Lay of Kraka. New York: The American-Scandinavian Foundation, 1964 (reprint of 1930 edition).*

Senn, Harry A., Were-Wolf and Vampire in Romania. Boulder, Colorado: East European Monographs, 1982.

Simpson, Jacqueline, Icelandic Folktales and Legends. Berkeley: University of California Press, 1972.*

Stevenson, John, Yoshitoshi's Thirty-Six Ghosts. New York: Weather-hill/Blue Tiger, 1983.*

Summers, Montague:
The Vampire: His Kith and Kin. New Hyde Park, New York: University Books, 1960.* ·
The Vampire in Europe. New Hyde Park, New York: University Books, 1968.*
The Werewolf. New Hyde Park, New York: University Books, 1966.*

* Titles marked with an asterisk were especially helpful in the preparation of this volume.

# Acknowledgments

The editors are particularly indebted to John Dorst, consultant, for his assistance in the preparation of this volume.

The editors also wish to thank the following persons and institutions: François Avril, Curator, Département des Manuscrits, Bibliothèque Nationale, Paris; Piotr Błoński, Paris; John Christian, London; Peter Cormack, Deputy Keeper, William Morris Gallery, Walthamstow, Essex, England; Xavier Deryng, Paris; J. V. Earle, Keeper, Far Eastern Section, Victoria and Albert Museum, London; Rupert Faulkner, Far Eastern Section, Victoria and Albert Museum, London; Martin Forrest, Bourne Fine Art, Edinburgh, Scotland; Marielise Göpel, Archiv für Kunst und Geschichte, West Berlin; Jean Grenyer, Sime Memorial Gallery, Worplesdon, Surrey, England; Kenichiro Hashimoto, Yokohama; Dieter Hennig, Director, Brüder-Grimm-Museum, Kassel, Germany; Christine Hofmann, Bayerische Staatsgemäldesammlungen, Munich; G. Irvine, Department of Oriental Antiquities, British Museum, London; Heidi Klein, Bildarchiv Preussischer Kulturbesitz, West Berlin; Kunsthistorisches Institut der Universität, Bonn; Gabriele Mandel, Milan; Luisa Ricciarini, Milan; Lores Riva, Milan; B. W. Robinson, London; Mitsuhiko Shibata, Tokyo; Tessa Sidey, Assistant Keeper, Department of Fine Art, Birmingham Museum and Art Gallery, England; Evelyn Silber, Deputy Keeper, Department of Fine Art, Birmingham Museum and Art Gallery, England; Jinichi Suzuki, Tokyo.

## Chief Series Consultant

Tristram Potter Coffin, Professor of
English at the University of Pennsylvania, is a leading authority on folklore.
He is the author or editor of numerous
books and more than one hundred arti-
cles. His best-known works are *The British Traditional Ballad in North America, The
Old Ball Game, The Book of Christmas Folk-
lore* and *The Female Hero.*

This volume is one of a series that is based
on myths, legends and folk tales.

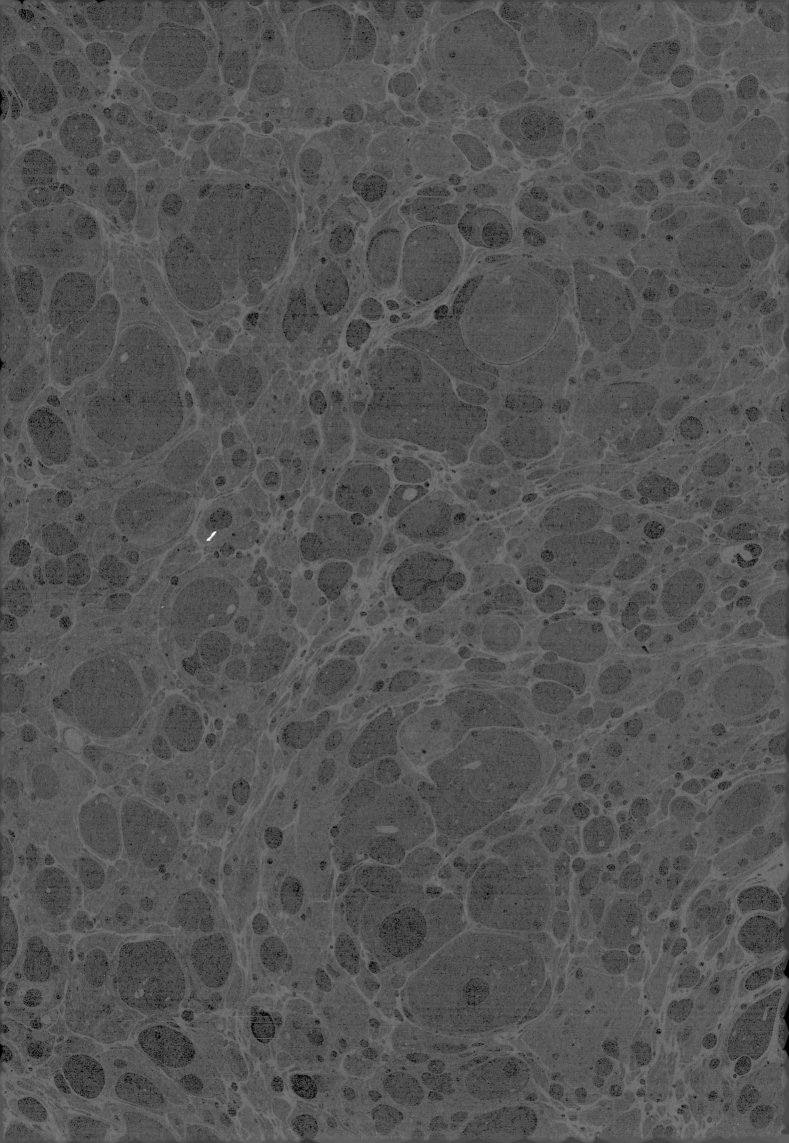